EDITOR IN CHIEF: A.K. CRUMP
EDITOR: STEPHANIE GREEN

PHOTOGRAPHY: CREDIT AND THANKS GOES TO ALL ACKNOWLEDGED PHOTOGRAPHERS, INCLUDING CHOCOLATE COMPANIES FEATURED HEREIN, AS WELL AS TO ALL ORGANIZATIONS AND INDIVIDUALS THAT CONTRIBUTED PHOTOGRAPHS TO THIS PUBLICATION.

SPECIAL THANKS TO THE CRUMP FAMILY, GEORGIA PETERSON DE MACHUCA, AND ROBERT GREEN. STEPHANIE GREEN CRUMP, ROB VALENCIA, THING 1 AND THING 2, AND TasteTV AND THE INTERNATIONAL CHOCOLATE SALON.

THE CHOCOLATE GUIDE

2008 Western Edition

tcb-cafe Publishing and media
PO Box 471706
San Francisco, California 94147
WWW.CAFEANDRE.COM
USA

Copyright © 2008, tcb-cafe Publishing and media

ISBN 0976768291
ISBN 978-09767682-9-6

THE CHOCOLATE
GUIDE

Contents

Intro

Southern California

Northern California

Nevada, Utah, Oregon, Washington, and British Columbia

Welcome to the 2008 Western Edition of our annual CHOCOLATE GUIDE!

With this edition, TCB-Cafe Publishing & Media, creators of the bestselling titles, THE CAFES OF SAN FRANCISCO, CHOCOLATE FRENCH, and THE FOOD OF FISHERMAN'S WHARF, launch the CHOCOLATE GUIDES.

These Guides are a new standalone concept in food & lifestyle publishing, aimed at a readership that believes the finer things in life are earned by looking for what you want, appreciating quality and skill, using the best ingredients, and enjoying good taste.

Each of these unique, stylish and valuable annual publications promotes 30-45 of a region's most appealing chocolatiers, chocolate makers, shops, boutiques, patisseries, cafes and retailers.

Many of the featured establishments are members of the International Chocolate Salon society, also founded by our team at TasteTV and Chocolate Television. All of the establishments represent the fabric of chocolate culture in their region, and support what we call, "The Chocolate Lifestyle."

We are very excited to bring this type of supportive and informative publication to our important and valued readers, and look forward to doing so for many years to come.

Publisher, A.K. Crump

Selections from L'Artisan du Chocolat,
Los Angeles

Chocolate Sounds

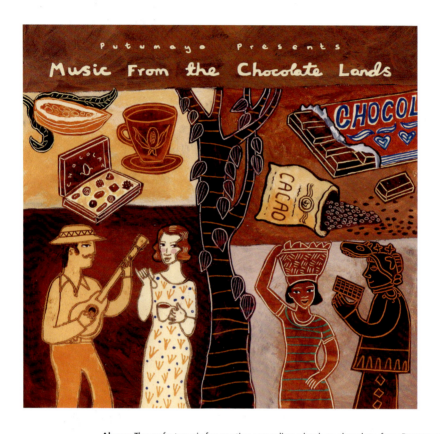

Above: The perfect music for creating or reading a book on chocolate, from Putumayo World Music. **Below:** Putumayo founders Dan Storper and Michael Kraus.

Chocolate Scents

Yosh Han, a perfumer in San Francisco combines the art of perfumery with aromachology, the therapeutic properties of essential oils. Her eponymous Luxury Elements Collections sells at Barneys New York and other specialty retailers.

Han also created **Temperare**, a collection of chocolate fragrances exclusively for what was formerly known as Temper Chocolates in Boston. The **Temperare** fragrance captures the essence of chocolate in a sensual, not sweet, perfume that is wearable by both women and men. Though not everyone will find themselves irresistible to the people around them, they will find that they are very pleasant to be around.

Yosh Han has seen her work appear in Vanity Fair, Town & Country, Bon Appétit, WSJ and Forbes. www.eaudeyosh.com

NEWTREE
NEWTREE
LAVENDER
LAVANDE
TRANQUILITY
SOOTHING/APAISANT
FINE BELGIAN MILK CHOCOLATE
FIN CHOCOLAT BELGE AU LAIT
MILK CHOCOLATE
MADE IN BELGIUM
NET WEIGHT/POIDS NET 2.82oz/

Love Chocolate? Take Your Pick

Fine chocolate ranges from healthy, imported and infused to organic, fair trade, and combined with fruits, herbs, spices and nuts.

TasteTV presents

The International
CHOCOLATE SALON

www.TasteTV.com

**San Francisco International
CHOCOLATE SALON**

The Chocolate Lifestyle

In the summer of 2007, TasteTV and its Chocolate Television program organized the first major chocolate show on the West Coast in two decades. The San Francisco International **CHOCOLATE SALON** was held on Bastille Day Weekend, July 14 and 15, 2007 in San Francisco. Chocolate aficionados, fanatics, buyers and journalists experienced the finest in artisan, gourmet & premium chocolate in one of the world's great culinary metropolitan areas.

The Salon drew over 2,000 attendees over the weekend, and highlights featured chocolate tasting, demonstrations, chef & author talks, wine pairings, chocolate painting, a chocolate spa and makeovers, and ongoing interviews by TasteTV's Chocolate Television program.

This event marked the launch of TasteTV's chocolate lifestyle brand, **ChocolateTelevision.com**. The launch included large and small scale Chocolate Salons in cities nationwide like San Francisco, Los Angeles, Las Vegas, Seattle, Miami, and New York. It also began the broadcast of Chocolate Television on major mobile cell phone carriers and on over 80 TV stations, as well as the publication of books such as **Chocolate French**, and **The Chocolate Guide**: To Chocolatiers, Chocolate Makers, Boutiques, Patisseries and Shops (2008 Western and Eastern Editions).

Chocolate Television is currently the only ongoing media brand dedicated 100% to the chocolate lifestyle. The program features chocolatier profiles, product reviews, interviews, tastings and wine pairings, events, and recipes. The Chocolate Guides support the Chocolate Lifestyle concept, promoting 35-50 of each region's most appealing chocolatiers, chocolate makers, shops, boutiques, patisseries, cafes and retailers.

Updates on the Chocolate Lifestyle can be found at the following websites:
Chocolate Television: www.ChocolateTelevision.com
San Francisco International Chocolate Salon: www.SFChocolateSalon.com
Los Angeles International Chocolate Salon: www.LAChocolateSalon.com
Seattle International Chocolate Salon: www.SeattleChocolateSalon.com
Miami International Chocolate Salon: www.MiamiChocolateSalon.com
The International Chocolate Salon: www.InternationalChocolateSalon.com
Singles Chocolate Salon: www.SinglesChocolateSalon.com
Bridal Chocolate Salon: www.BridalChocolateSalon.com

CHOCOLATE TELEVISION

Enjoy the Chocolate Lifestyle

Available on cable, video on demand, mobile cell phones and
as video podcasts.
For more information, go to

www.ChocolateTelevision.com

Clockwise from top left: Skagen of Denmark watch in chocolate, Traditional Mexican Hot Chocolate bar from CocoaConnoisseur.com, Le Creuset enameled cast iron Oval Dutch Oven in Chocolate, Chocolate Tahitian Pearl Necklace from the Pearl Outlet and other locations, Sherry Baby Orchids smell like chocolate - from hawaiianmagic.net, Wilton Chocolate Pro Electric Melting Pot

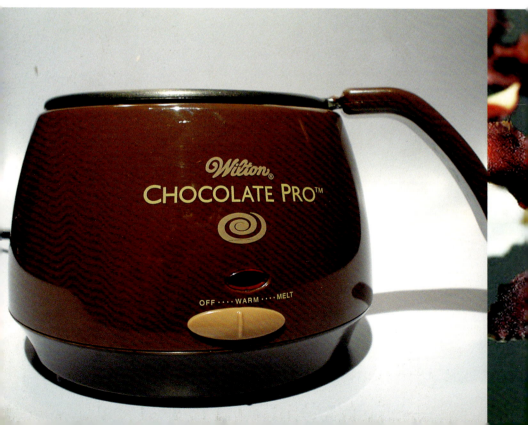

Gear for the Chocolate Lifestyle

Marr, Old Vine Zinfandel, Mattern Ranch, Mendocino County

Vintner: This wine is a bit rustic and meaty, dominated by aromas of Bing cherries, blackberries and ripe plums, which are tinged with white pepper and hints of minerals, with a deep, full mouthfeel on the palate.

SFS: Not as robust as some Zinfandels, but definitely a pleasing wine to enjoy.

Cuvée Patrick, Marr Cellars, Petite Sirah

Vintner: The nose and palate feature a combination of brighter red fruit (raspberries and strawberries) and a wisp of rose petals, along with dense, darker fruit of ripe blackberries and plums, with a touch of brown spices.

Us: We tend to be quite fond of all of the Marr wines, this one included. A great value for the price.

Foppiano, Zinfandel, Dry Creek

Vintner: Offers a huge structure with deep, rich purple color, complex aromas of spices and black pepper, concentrated flavors of ripe berries and chocolate from the inviting nose to a rich, silky finish.

Us: A good value wine, and worth including in your monthly wine selection.

Silkwood, Cabernet-Syrah, Red Duet, Stanislaus County

Vintner: This specially selected 50-50 blend of Cabernet and Syrah from their vineyards is extraordinary smooth on the back palate, and is designed for most women who prefer a smooth finish.

Us: An exotic hybrid that well merits its Silver Medal awards.

Mumm, 25th Anniversary Brut Reserve, Napa Valley,

Vintner: The Mumm Napa 25th Anniversary Reserve Brut ($25) celebrates the founding of the winery in a reserve-style bottling that combines the finest Napa Valley fruit with traditional "methode champenoise" wine-making techniques.

SFS: Some people wait for occasions to drink champagne, but with the Brut Reserve we figure "because you want to" is as good as any.

Foppiano Estate Bottled Petite Sirah, Russian River Valley

Vintner: The style pursued by Foppiano is one of forward, aggressive, glorious fruitiness; with toasty oak aromas further enhance the wine's complexity. Luscious black berry fruit dominates this Foppiano wine.

Us: "Spicy and delicious."

Steele Wines Pinot Noir Caneros

Vintner: Carneros Pinot Noir is a flavorful, layered, versatile wine with universal appeal. This has been confirmed by its inclusion in the Wine Spectator's "Top 100 Wines of the Year" in several vintages. The wine shows strawberry and cherry preserves in the nose and on the palate along with well-integrated hints of oak, vanilla, and cassis.

Us: Try it with chocolate!

2005
Sol Rouge
MARSANNE · ROUSSANNE
NORTH COAST

Sol Rouge Winery

Quady Winery

Quady Winery

VERMEER DUTCH CHOCOLATE CREAM POUND CAKE

1. Preheat oven to 325 F. Use 8.5" x 4.5" x 2.5" metal loaf pan to trace and cut out a rectangle of wax paper. Butter the loaf pan and insert wax paper at bottom of pan. Butter the wax paper.

2. Melt chocolate squares in a small heatproof bowl over hot – but not simmering – water. Stir occasionally. Remove from heat and set aside.

3. In another bowl, combine flour, baking soda, baking powder and salt. Set aside. Cream butter and sugar in large bowl with an electric mixer. Beat until light and fluffy, about 3 minutes. Beat in the cooled chocolate, then the eggs – one at a time – and the vanilla.

4. Stir in half the flour mixture. Then stir in the sour cream. Then stir in remaining flour. Quickly stir in the Vermeer Dutch Chocolate Cream Liqueur (shake the Vermeer well before pouring).

5. Scrape batter into prepared pan and smooth the top. Bake 50-55 minutes or until toothpick inserted into the middle of the cake comes out clean.

6. Cool in the pan on a rack for ten minutes. Remove cake from pan, and peel wax paper from bottom. Let cool completely.

7. Fill bottom of pan with " Vermeer Dutch Chocolate Cream Liqueur (shake the Vermeer well before pouring). Put cake back in pan and allow Vermeer to soak in.

Glaze:
1. Sift confectioner's sugar into a bowl. Using electric mixer beat in Vermeer Dutch Chocolate Cream Liqueur (shake the Vermeer well before pouring). Mix until smooth and thin (about 2 minutes). Drizzle glaze over top of the cooled cake, smoothing with knife when necessary and allowing glaze to drip down the sides of the cake.

Serving Suggestion:
Serve with vanilla ice cream that has been drizzled with Vermeer Dutch Chocolate Cream Liqueur

Cake Ingredients:

3 oz unsweetened chocolate

8 tablespoons unsalted butter, softened

1 cup bleached all-purpose flour

1 cup sugar

1 teaspoon baking soda

2 eggs

1 teaspoon baking powder

1 teaspoon vanilla

1 teaspoon salt
1 cup sour cream

1/8 cup Vermeer Dutch Chocolate Cream Liqueur

For the Glaze:

1 cup confectioner's sugar

3 tablespoons Vermeer Dutch Chocolate Cream Liqueur

Recipe courtesy of Vermeer and Elizabeth Colie Gadberry.

THE CHOCOLATE GUIDE TO SOUTHERN CALIFORNIA & MEXICO

Nestle Chocolate Museum
Mexico

Nestle Chocolate Museum
Mexico City (Paseo Tollocan near Toluca)
Mexico
Designed by Rojkind Arquitectos

Chuao Chocolatier

2345 Camino Vida Roble   Carlsbad   CA   92011   1.888.635.1414
www.chuaochocolatier.com

Sometimes really nice people do succeed, and we're certainly happy that Chuao is among those who have. Chuao Chocolatier is Southern California's exclusive Venezuelan artisan chocolatier. The name stems from the legendary cacao-producing region of Chuao (pronounced chew-WOW) located in central Venezuela. Chuao Chocolatier blends European confection techniques with premium Venezuelan chocolate and all natural ingredients to produce fine handmade chocolates. The most popular Chuao product is currently the Spicy Maya bar. Chuao Chocolatier offers creations such as Hot Chocolate inspired by the ancient recipe of the Mayas; the Modena, a dark chocolate bonbon filled with a blend of strawberry caramel and balsamic vinegar; and the signature Picante ChocoPod, a California raisin fondue in a Napa Valley Cabernet caramel, spiced with Pasilla chili and cayenne pepper.

Founded by Master Chocolatier Michael Antonorsi, for him and brother Richard this is a part of their heritage. In 2002, Master Chocolatier Michael Antonorsi launched Chuao Chocolatier in San Diego County to arouse the senses of Southern Californians with an unusual, unexpected and delicious flavor experience that can only come from the world's best imported chocolate. Michael dreamed of opening up a unique chocolate boutique that beautifully blended modern-day innovations with his Venezuelan family traditions and moved his family from Venezuela to Paris. He studied at the Ecolé Superieure de Cuisine Francaise Ferrandi in Paris where he gained certification as a French Chef and also completed specialized training in Pastry and Chocolaterie at the Ecolé Lenotré.

Where to buy: Chuao has a number of boutique locations throughout Southern California and soon in Florida. Chuao Chocolatier offers their products nationwide through specialty stores and gourmet retailers such as Whole Foods.

Chuao Chocolatier

Mignon Chocolate

315 N. Verdugo Road   Glendale   CA   91206   818-549-9600
www.MignonChocolate.com

Mignon means "sweet and cute" in French, and Mignon Chocolate has both sweet international chocolate roots and sweet international chocolate flair. Their Glendale location has a European style atmosphere with a cafe seating area, a large patio, and two very large display cases filled with over 60 different type of chocolates and desserts. The chocolates are primarily hand-molded pieces using over 65 different flavors and combinations. Some of the most popular flavors are orange peel stripes dipped in dark chocolates, Delis Squares, Peanut Pralines, and Hazelnut cups.

Mignon is a 3rd generation chocolatier, owned and operated by the Terpoghossian family. They create their chocolates and truffles based on secret family recipes used in their two boutiques on two continents. Their original location of 70 years is in Tehran, Iran (in the early 1970's, Mignon was known among Iranians and all minorities as the "King of Chocolate" in Tehran). The second Mignon location is in California. Both of these boutiques offer a European atmosphere by serving coffee drinks and high-end handmade chocolates and gourmet truffles. Mignon also provides chocolate fountains to customers and local hotels and caterers, as well as offers custom chocolate party favors and luxurious gift boxes.

It goes without saying that Mignon has a Hollywood following, including celebs like Adam Sandler, Arnold Schwarzenegger, and local news personalities and politicians. They also cater for many Hollywood celebrities at private parties, at award nights, and on other occasions.

Mignon Chocolate
Glendale, California

Yum!

Southern California   www.yum.tv

Yum! specializes in Superfoods -- foods that are super tasty and super healthy. Yum! was founded by Koina Freeman, an award-winning filmmaker and chef who has worked in both London and Hong Kong. Because chocolate's health benefits have been prized for hundreds of years, Koina painstakingly searches the world for the purest ingredients to handcraft her chocolates. From wild Tibetan Goji berries to premium Ecuadorean cacao, all of the farmers are Fair Trade and Certified Organic. Yum's handcrafted chocolates are completely raw, vegan, and organic. The Ecuadorean Cacao is Fair Trade, wheat free, gluten-free, soy-free, dairy-free and diabetic friendly and sweetened only with premium raw blue agave and never processed sugars. Their vanilla beans are from Madagascar and not from a bottle.

The most popular Yum! products are the Chocolate Goo (spread it or ooze it on anything or just scoop it from the jar) which comes in a Wild Cinnamon, Japanese Green Tea, and Bombay Curry. Also, the popular Shaolin Goji Bar is made with Wild Tibetan Goji berries, and the Peppermint Haze Bar is made with imported Hemp seeds. Celebrities that have tried Yum! include one of the Olsen twins, Heather McCartney, and actress Kirsten Dunst.

Asia is a great influence on Koina's work, from her Shaolin Goji bars to the Black Pearl truffles made with real Japanese Wasabi. The Sea Monkey bar is made with blue green algae and premium Japanese Matcha. Says Koina: When I began selling my chocolates I had no idea how popular they would be, but one day my car broke down and my neighbor had to drive me to make my delivery. I was several hours late and figured no one would notice or care. But when we arrived the store manager announced over the loud-speaker that Yum Tum was here and I was mobbed by several dozen hungry fans. My neighbor shrieked, "Wow its like being with a celebrity!" I beamed with pride, "Me?!?" "No." She said, "The chocolate!"

Where to buy: Yum! can be found in select Whole Foods markets in Southern California and Erewhon natural market. New locations are continuously being added, so please check http://yum.tv often.

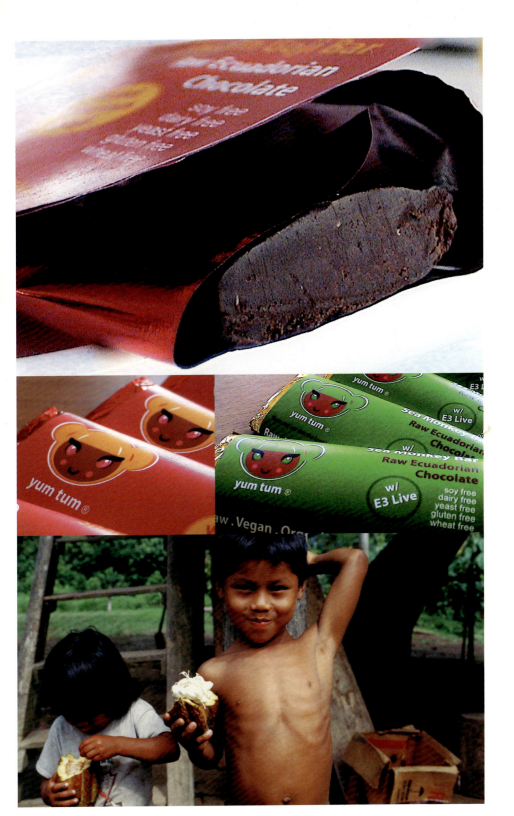

L'Artisan du Chocolat

3364 West First Street   Los Angeles   CA 90004   310-880-9396
www.lartisanduchocolat.com

Christian and Whajung Alexandre are so charming that they make you want to taste their already irresistible confections. L' Artisan du Chocolat is set in a cute little European-style boutique where customers enjoy the smell of fresh chocolate while watching the Maitre Chocolatiers create new indulgences.

This family owned enterprise makes French chocolates fresh every day using traditional methods and not adding any preservatives or over-adding sugar. They currently hand make around 80 different chocolates that range from the classic line of French chocolates to more unusual flavors, including some quite "edgy" pieces (Chili, Cucumber, Garlic etc.). Whatever they make, the duo wins praises and awards everywhere, including at the 2007 San Francisco International Chocolate Salon.

Popular pieces include truffles, Pave Noir 72, 3 Chili/Apricot, Rose Petal, Lavender, and Mango-Wasabi. A sample of international celebrities who have tasted their work includes First Lady of California Maria Shriver, The Dalai Lama, Duchess of York Sarah Fergusson, Huell Howser, and author/TV host Suze Orman.

Where to buy: The L'Artisan shop and selected gourmet stores and wine places along with Hotels, Restaurants, Casino in Las Vegas. Gift basket companies and many corporations for their annual corporate gifts, including large French and American banks in California and Oregon.

L'Artisan du Chocolat
Los Angeles, California

Ojai Chocolat

1010 Mercer Ave.   Ojai   CA   93023   805-646-0454
www.chilihot-chocolat.com

Says Ojai Chocolat founder Mimi Milme, "We have taken the 'Food of the Gods' and made it into everyone's Food!" Organic Vegan Chocolates are what you find with Ojai Chocolat, created for "those who love the pure essence of what real chocolate naturally is, and what it does for them mentally and physically."

Without the sugar and dairy to which many people are allergic or sensitive, Ojai Chocolat is made with only the organic raw chocolate nibs and sweetened with wild crafted Agave (in order not to spike glucose levels). Nothing artificial is ever added. Only vanilla beans and essential oils, roots and pods are used. Some of the chocolates designed with roots and proteins from the Andes are made for energy and hormonal balance. In addition, athletes use the Ojai Chocolat bars called 'Raw Stamina' for energy.

'Raw Stamina' is Maca rich. Maca is a root that is said to help eliminate hot flashes and other menopausal symptoms in women. It also is believed to induce testosterone production in men that increases libido and boosts their sexual drive.

The bar's end results therefore support chocolate's long reputation for sexually stimulating men and women.

Founder Mimi Milne, having received acclaim for her dancing and designing; traveled the world belly dancing as 'Mabrooka.' She designed and manufactured a California clothing line called Mabrooka Originals, and later created a company called Whitebird, (www.whitebirdsalt.com) specializing in Celtic Sea Salts for internal and external health and beauty. Having her own sensitivities to sugars and dairy , as well as being a healthy gourmet cook, Mimi developed Ojai Chocolat. Inspired by the movie 'Chocolat,' her first chocolate product was 'Chili*Hot Chocolat,' a seasoned cocoa powder to be mixed as a hot cocoa drink or used as a spice (giving way to the website www.chilihot-chocolat.com).

Ojai's chocolates, without sugar or dairy, are satisfying for both discriminating chocolate lovers and raw food disciples.

Boule, L.A.'s Modern Patisserie
420 N. La Cienega Boulevard
Los Angeles, CA 90048
310-289-9977
www.boulela.com

John Kelly Chocolates
Los Angeles, CA
800.609.4243
www.johnkellychocolates.com

Valerie Confections
3360 West First Street
Los Angeles, CA 90004
213.739.8149
www.valerieconfections.com

Our toffees ar
handmade in sma
batches, using th
highest qualit
ingredien

Chocolatt
12008 Wilshire Blvd.
West Los Angeles, CA 90025
888.808.8548
www.chocolatt.com

Madame Chocolat
212 North Canon Drive
Beverly Hills, CA 90210
310.247.9912
www.madame.chocolat.com

Chalmers Chocolate
1119 Colorado Avenue Ste. 17
Santa Monica, CA 90401
310.451.3717
www.chalmersganache.com

Crown City Confections
1800 Carnegie Avenue
Santa Ana, CA 92705
949.660.9581

Victorian Chocolate Molds

P.O. Box 901 / 700 Third St.   San Juan Bautista, CA 95045   (831) 623 1681   www.VictorianChocolateMolds.Com

Author Wendy Mullen collects and provides for purchase thousands of antique chocolate molds. According to her, these are molds that can and should be used for creating art in chocolate and various other mediums.

Wendy's antique chocolate molds have a wide following, including Disney and artists such as Robert Twardzik, whose confectionery design studio creates sumptuous wedding & party cakes, petit fours, chocolates and other pastries & confections for special occasions. Twardzik has been seen on Oprah and the Food Network. His work has also been featured in Wendy's book project, "Antique European Chocolate Molds."

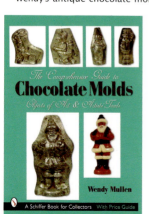

The molds Mullens collects have a distinct European influence, and she has procured over 50,000 designs for the collection. Her expertise on the topic has provided fertile ground for the 2 books she has written, as well as features in the Better Homes Santa Claus Book. Her most popular title is "The Comprehensive Guide to Chocolate Molds-Objects of Art and Artists' Tools."

Wendy notes that holidays themes are particularly popular for mold collectors, especially the Christmas and Easter antique chocolate molds.

Where to buy: VictorianChocolateMolds.Com and at fairs, author talks, etc.

Marceline's Chocolate
Disneyland

CARAMEL CHOCOLATE
MARSHMALLOWS $3.00

CANDY MADE
EXCLUSIVELY
AT THE
Disneyland
RESORT

CHOCOLATE WALNUT

Qzina Specialty Foods

16625 Saticoy Street   Van Nuys   CA   91406   818-787-2000
www.qzina.com

Let's say you want to start a chocolate shop or become a pastry chef. In that case it's always a good idea to know where you can source quality products. Qzina Specialty Foods is a national importer and distributor of premium imported and domestic products for the pasty and bakery industry. Qzina has offices in 8 locations around North America, including Miami, Los Angeles, Chicago, San Francisco, New Jersey, Edmonton, Toronto and Vancouver.

As a premier importer of chocolate products, Qzina supplies a number of items, including: fine chocolate from Belgium, France and Switzerland; mousse cake bases and dessert pastes from Germany; jams and glazes from Belgium; frozen fruit purees from France; domestic fruit fillings; delicate chocolate cups and decorations from Holland and the U.S. market; chocolate and marzipan decorations from Germany; chocolate transfers from Germany and

Belgium; specialty products and alcoholic pastry flavors from France; tart shells and puff pastries from Belgium, France and Holland; truffles and pralines from Germany; specialty bread and baking mixes from Germany and the domestic market; and numerous domestic and international specialty products such as flavors, extracts, stabilizers, etc.

Fine chocolate products that Qzina carries are high-end selections such as Chocoa, Callebaut, Valrhona, Michel Cluizel, Suchard and Schokinag. Qzina also offers Chocolate Classes at each of our location, hosted by their Corporate Pastry Chef.

Chuao Chocolatier
937 S. Coast Highway 101 Suite
C-109
Encinitas
CA

Leonidas Belgian Chocolates
201 N Larchmont Blvd
Los Angeles
CA

Chocolate M
747 S Kingsley Dr
Los Angeles
CA

Chocolate
1120 Santee St
Los Angeles
CA

Rocky Mountain Chocolate Factory
927 Broxton Ave
Los Angeles
CA

Happy Chocolates
4159 Wanda Dr.
Los Angeles
CA

Hollywood Jack's Chocolates
5660 Hollywood Blvd
Los Angeles
CA

Mr Marcel Gourmet Market
6333 W Third St
Los Angeles
CA

Littlejohn's English Toffee
6333 W 3RD St Ste 432
Los Angeles
CA

Garvey Nut & Candy
6416 Flotilla St
Los Angeles
CA

Aaron Lindgren Chocolates
912 South Barrington Avenue
Los Angeles
CA
310.207.3131

Candy Alley
13020 San Vicente Blvd
Los Angeles
CA

Comparte's Chocolatier
912 S Barrington Ave
Los Angeles
CA

K Chocolatier Brentwood
11677 San Vicente Blvd Ste
111
Los Angeles
CA

Candy Bouquet
12900 Venice Blvd
Los Angeles
CA

Chocolate Sun
12501 Appleton Way
Los Angeles
CA
(310) 390-8007

Monsieur Marcel
Third & Fairfax
Los Angeles
CA
(323) 939-7792

Picholine Chocolatier
3360 W 1st St
Los Angeles
CA
(213) 252-8722

Angelina
430 N Bedford Dr
Beverly Hills
CA

Teuscher Chocolates & Cafe
9548 Brighton Way
Beverly Hills
CA
(310) 276-2776

Edelweiss Chocolates
444 N Canon Dr
Beverly Hills
CA

Lee Gelfond Chocolate
275 S Robertson Blvd Ste B
Beverly Hills
CA

Kchocolatier Factory
9897 Santa Monica Blvd
Beverly Hills
CA
(310) 286-9300

Sakuraya
16134 S Western Ave
Gardena
CA

Hawaiian Host Chocolates
15601 S Avalon Blvd
Gardena
CA

In tem pe ran tia
15324 Antioch Street
Pacific Palisades
CA
310.459.4703

Mike's Chocolates
712 Deep Valley Dr
Rolling Hills Estates
CA

Jin Patisserie
1202 Abbot Kinney Blvd
Venice
CA

Leonidas Chocolate Cafe
331 Santa Monica Blvd
Santa Monica
CA

Imperial Nougat Co
12035 Slauson Ave Ste C
Santa Fe Springs
CA

Ambala Sweets
18433 Pioneer Blvd
Artesia
CA

Bon Bon
6346 E Pacific Coast Hwy
Long Beach
CA

Chocolate Box
4123 Norse Way
Long Beach
CA

Chocolate Box Cafe
714 Foothill Blvd
La Canada
CA
(818) 790-7918

Violet's Cakes
21 E Holly St
Pasadena
CA

Ghirardelli Soda Fountain and
Chocolate Shop
110 W Colorado Blvd
Pasadena
CA

Leonidas
49 W. Colorado Boulevard
Pasadena
CA
(626) 577-7121

Chocolate Covered Company
P.O. Box 40121
Pasadena
CA
877-347-7332

House of Chocolates
7801 Alabama Ave Ste 3
Canoga Park
CA

Kelly's Coffee & Fudge Factory
9301 Tampa Ave
Northridge
CA

Chocolate Covered Company
6860 Canby Ave.
Reseda
CA

Sweet Candy
370 W Hillcrest Dr
Thousand Oaks
CA

World's Best Toffee
22440 Cypress Pl
Santa Clarita
CA

Ultimate Confections
10665 Vanowen St.
Burbank
CA
(800) 767-5259

Fudge Fatale
12424 1/2 Ventura Blvd
Studio City
CA

Designer Chocolates
12643 Sherman Way Ste O
North Hollywood
CA
(818) 982-9106

Candy Factory
12508 Magnolia Blvd
North Hollywood
CA

Mercado Chocolate
100 Universal City Plz
Universal City
CA

Very Special Chocolates Incorporated
760 N McKeever Ave
Azusa
CA

A Kline Chocolatier
210 W 2nd St
Claremont
CA

Chocolate Florist
133 1/2 N Glendora Ave
Glendora
CA

Halgrens
1206 N. Grove Ave
Ontario
CA
(909) 986-4836

Creative Chocolate
1324 Peppertree Cir
West Covina
CA

Sweet Annie's Chocolates
109 W Main St
Alhambra
CA

LOCAL DIRECTORY

Chocolate Maker
295 D St # 3
Chula Vista
CA
(619) 427-5707

Chocolate Palace
135 Landis Ave
Chula Vista
CA

Centifonti Chocolates & Gifts
8209 La Mesa Blvd
La Mesa
CA

Truffles
7857 Girard Ave
La Jolla
CA

Give Chocolate
1808 Cedar Street
Ramona
CA
(760) 788-9220

Chi Chocolat
2021 India Street
San Diego
CA
(619) 501-9215

The Sweet Life
1484 Garnet Ave.
San Diego
CA

San Diego Chocolate Field
3941 Mason St Ste 1
San Diego
CA

Arlene's Gourmet Toffee's
11545 Sorrento Valley Rd
San Diego
CA

A Chocolatier
4370 La Jolla Village Drive
San Diego
CA
(858) 755-1600

Chuao Chocolate Cafe
4465 La Jolla Village Dr
San Diego
CA

Yoku Moku USA
PO Box 26879
San Diego
CA

Van Valkenburg Chocolates
73-655 El Paseo Suite J
Palm Desert
CA

Heminger's Fudge & Chocolates
Inc
211 S Palm Canyon Dr
Palm Springs
CA
(760) 416-0075

The Chocolate Florist
40477 Murrieta Hot Springs Rd.
Murrieta
CA
(909)677-1268

California Candy Creations
31 Fortune Dr
Irvine
CA

Bodega Chocolates
3333 Bristol Street Suite 2830
Costa Mesa
CA
714-432-0708

Bon Bon Sticky Fingers
1875 Newport Blvd Ste 203
Costa Mesa
CA

Sprinkles Cupcakes
944 Avocado Ave
Newport Beach
CA

Helen Grace Chocolates
1124 Irvine Ave
Newport Beach
CA

Not Just Candy
600 E Bay Ave
Newport Beach
CA

Schmid's Fine Chocolates
99 Avenida Del Mar
San Clemente
CA
949.369.1052

Reefcandy
7010 Trask Ave
Westminster
CA

Chocolate Angel
1104 N Olive St
Santa Ana
CA

Helen Grace Chocolates
3313 S Bristol St
Santa Ana
CA

Bodega Chocolates
17290 Newhope St
Fountain Valley
CA

Simply Scrumptious Confections
1971 Irvine Blvd
Tustin
CA

Candy Man Incorporated
1181 N Blue Gum St
Anaheim
CA

Tea With Alice Chocolatiers
PO Box 5761
Anaheim
CA

Helen Grace Chocolates
1044 Brea Mall
Brea
CA

Island Snacks Incorporated
393 N Cypress St
Orange
CA

Chocolate Delight
326 W Katella Ave
Orange
CA

Bon Bon International
20 City Blvd W
Orange
CA

Sweets from Heaven
20 City Blvd W
Orange
CA

Confection Affections
2959 Rochester Cir
Corona
CA

Helen Grace Chocolates
650 S Lincoln Ave
Corona
CA

Trufflehound's Fine Chocolates
607 E Main St Ste E
Ventura
CA

Confectionately Yours
2855 Johnson Dr
Ventura
CA

Kangaroo Gold Chocolate
530 Spectrum Cir
Oxnard
CA

Isle of Chocolate
547 W Channel Islands Blvd
Port Hueneme
CA

Amadeus Fine Chocolate &
Coffee
537 State St
Santa Barbara
CA
(805) 966-6969

Chocolate Gallery
5705 Calle Real
Goleta
CA

Chocolate Maya
15 W Gutierrez St
Santa Barbara
CA
(805) 965-5956

Sweet Creations Chocolate Shop
621 E Ocean Ave
Lompoc
CA

Ingeborg's Homemade Chocolates
1679 Copenhagen Dr
Solvang
CA

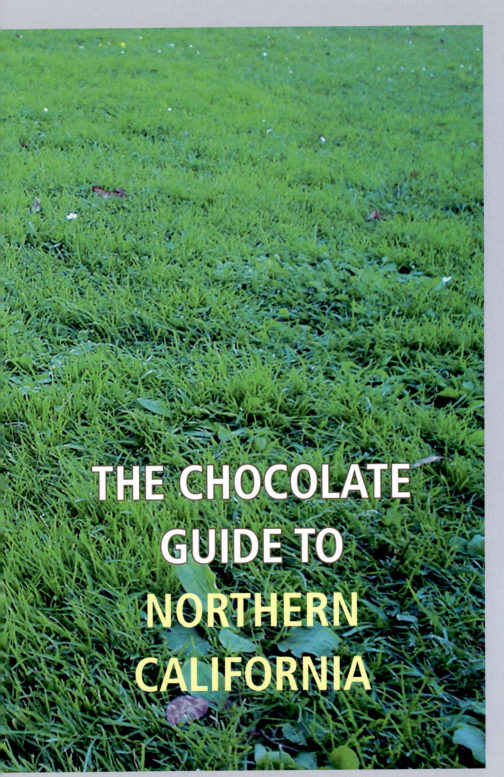

THE CHOCOLATE GUIDE TO NORTHERN CALIFORNIA

The Truffle Shop
DeGroot's Desserts

408 Broad St. Suite #2   Nevada City   CA   95959   800-366-3538
www.chocolategod.com

Cake lovers, dessert lovers, chocolate lovers, Nevada City awaits! The Truffle Shop is your destination, a quaint European style Dessert Cafe with a playful "under the ocean" theme above the dessert cases. The Truffle Shop is also a retail business featuring the chocolate creations of Chef Willam DeGroot.

Now in its 20th year of business, the Truffle Shop is located in Nevada City, one hour northeast of Sacramento, in the Sierra Foothills of Northern California. Their specialty is Chocolate Truffles and Truffle Torts made with imported Belgian chocolate and using the finest liqueurs.

The DeGroot collection of 22 truffles is the shop's most popular product, and the DeGroot Chocolate Oblivion Torte comes in second place. Some well-known faces who have visited include President Bill Clinton and Senator Hillary Clinton, Pope Paul II, and Clint Walker.

Where to buy: The primary location is in Nevada City. In San Francisco you can find the DeGroot line of truffles at the Chocolate Covered store in the Noe Valley neighborhood.

The DeGroot Truffle Selection

The Truffle Shop / DeGroot's Desserts
Nevada City, California

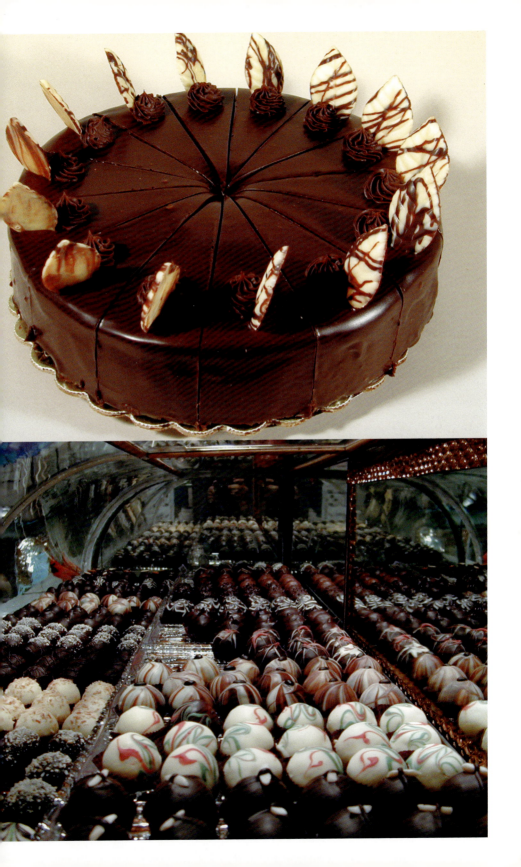

Left: Etienne Guittard
Below: Gary Guittard

CHOCOLATE WITH HISTORY

Guittard Chocolate Company
Burlingame, California

Founded in 1868 on the San Francisco waterfront by Etienne Guittard, the Guittard Chocolate Company is a family affair. The firm has passed from father to son for generations. With this inheritance has come a true love for chocolate making. This love is translated into a personal attention to their products and a tradition of French methods.

Guittard has several product lines. The premium line is the E. Guittard Collection, named after founder Etienne. The E. Guittard Collection is based on the original handwritten recipes of Etienne, well before the days of chocolate mass production and over-sweetening. The collection includes both blends and single bean varietal chocolates. Guittard sources many of the single-bean varietals for the E. Guittard collection from plantations in Venezuela, Colombia and Equador. These plantations are familiar with the Guittard's heirloom methods, including bean fermentation and drying procedures. Later, the beans are French roasted, crushed into nibs and hulled, stone ground, refined into a thick paste, conched to give it a silky texture, and then tempered and molded. At each stage of the process the chocolate is constantly tasted, guaranteeing a high quality equaling that found in France.

In addition to the single-bean varietals, the E. Guittard collection includes bean blends. Guittard is lauded for its 64% L'Harmonie dark chocolate bars, characterized by light floral aromas and a clean, deep finish. Guittard also has a popular 38% milk chocolate known as Soleil d'Or.

Guittard chocolate products are also widely used as the base chocolate by several well-known chocolatiers, as well as highly prized by chefs and restaurants across North America.

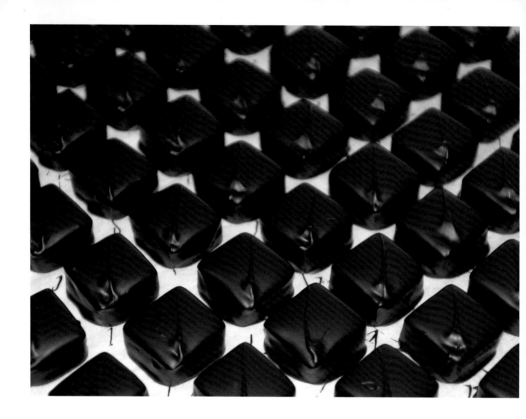

Pieces of Heaven Fine Chocolates

3686 The Barnyard Carmel CA 93923 831-625-3368

Names often carry meaning, and this shop's name says it all. Pieces of Heaven has been making fine chocolates by hand since 1987 and has become the premier chocolate shop in the Carmel Valley / Central Coast area of California. They make a full array or assorted chocolates including 24 different truffles, 8 fudges, many nut clusters and barks, caramel nut clusters, buttery English Toffee, soft chewy caramels and butter creams, and caramel apples.

Owners Robert and Peggy Whitted have each been in the chocolate business for 21 years. They attended the RCI Candy School in Erie, PA and qualified for the Master Chocolatier with Retail Confectioners International. They also attend numerous conventions and seminars to hone and expand their skills.

Pieces of Heaven is also an old fashioned candy store. They cook and dip all the assorted candy by hand, it is not molded or enrobed by machine, making each piece unique and fresh. At the shop, the public can enjoy watching the entire process through the large front windows. Celebrities who have tasted their products include Doris Day and Clint and Dina Eastwood (plus Clint's resorts).

Says the Whitted's: A couple from San Francisco came on a mission--his mother was terminally ill and her last request was to have some Pieces of Heaven truffles. Wow!

Where to buy: At the retail location in the Barnyard Shopping Village at the mouth of Carmel Valley.

Decadent Tastes
L'Estasi Dolce

1400 Pico Ave.   Pacific Grove   CA   93950   831.643.0908
www.decadenttastes.com

Once you taste these chocolates, you may wonder if 'decadence' has been redefined as 'awesome.'

Founded by Rose Ramos-Benzel, her Filipino Chinese American heritage influences the Decadent Tastes' flavor profiles. Rose's motto is simple and elegant, keeping flavors subtle but sublime.

Decadent Tastes specializes in Asian-Fusion confections, combining traditional Oriental spices with popular European and American ingredients. The result is a unique taste experience with layers of complexity for the discriminating palate. The company also offers a series of gourmet wine truffles.

The Asian-Fusion line is hand-crafted from family recipes, using high-quality natural ingredients. Gourmet chocolates include the signature Peanut Ginger Chocolate, Lemongrass Ginger, Praline Ginger and Mint Ginger Truffles. Caramel corns in this collection are Sesame Almond and Maple Almond Caramel Corn.

At the 2007 San Francisco International Chocolate Salon, the Lemongrass Ginger Truffles samples were devoured, and inventory sold out within hours of the first day. Other popular choices are the Cabernet Truffles, Port Truffles, and Maple Almond Caramel Corn.

Says Rose: Our first product on the market, our signature Peanut Ginger Chocolate was our family holiday chocolate. In 2003 my husband and I decided to give them out as gifts. We knew we had something special when we got calls from people raving about them; we even had one person tell me he'd pay me to make him some more! Thus, the business was born.

Where to buy: Dean & Deluca in St. Helena, the Piedmont Grocery in Oakland, Draeger's in Northern California, Piazza's Fine Foods (Palo Alto & San Mateo, CA), Gene's Fine Foods (Saratoga, CA), the Pebble Beach Market.

Fleur de Cocoa

39 N. Santa Cruz Ave.   Los Gatos   CA   95030   408-354-3574
www.fleurdecocoa.com

Fleur de Cocoa is an authentic, upscale French pastry and chocolate shop in downtown Los Gatos. Only fresh, high quality ingredients (and only French chocolate) are used, and everything is made on site. Fleur de Cocoa offers beautiful French pastries ranging from classics such as tangy lemon curd tartes, crispy milles-feuilles, chocolate éclairs and an assortment of breakfast croissants to decadent individual mousse cakes with Chef Janvier's contemporary flair. The popular lunch menu includes quiches, croque-monsieur sandwiches, French tuna sandwiches and salad, and other specialties. The café is small, with just 18 seats, but bustles with locals, tourists, and those who drive the distance to get quality French items. In addition, Chef Janvier makes his own chocolate candies and, during the warmer months, ice creams and sorbets that remind the customers of the world famous Berthillon in Paris.

Master French Pastry Chef and Chocolatier Pascal Janvier and his wife Nicola are the sole owners of Fleur de Cocoa. Chef Janvier has been twice named One of America's Top 10 Pastry Chefs by Chocolatier/Pastry Art & Design magazine. He has won many competitions, including first place at the National Dessert Competition, and 3-time medalist at the US Pastry Team Competitions in 2001, 2003 and 2006. Chef Janvier is a member of the prestigious Academie Culinaire de France. When Chef Pascal Janvier was inducted into the Academie, his honorary godmother was Julia Child.

The most popular items at the shop are the Fleur de Cocoa chocolate - an extra-dark chocolate ganache filled candy, the Royal - a pastry made with almond sponge cake crowned with a crispy hazelnut praline layer and dark chocolate mousse, the Chocolat Chaud - homemade rich and silky dark hot chocolate, and the Macarons Parisiens.

Fleur de Cocoa
Los Gatos, California

Saratoga Chocolates

14572-B Big Basin Way   Saratoga   CA   95070   408-872-1431
www.saratogachocolates.com

Saratoga Chocolates makes passersby stop in their tracks. Everything looks so good, and is as good as it looks. The shop makes handmade confections using fresh local ingredients. The chocolate comes from two premier chocolate sources in California, the dairy is hormone free and they use locally grown nuts and fruits. The chocolate shop is beautifully appointed and resembles a small Parisian Chocolate Shop. A window from the shop looks into the Saratoga Chocolates production kitchen.

Saratoga Chocolates has two wonderful chocolatiers, including founder and owner Mary Loomas. Mary was self taught in chocolate and confections when she attended Ecole Chocolat and studied at Valhrona's chocolate school in France. Additionally they have a very talented chocolatier, Natascha Hoffmeyer, who attended the California Culinary Academy in San Francisco. The shop not only makes great chocolates, it also conducts a regular series of chocolate making courses for the home chef. Each class is 3.5 hours long. Students learn to make ganache, hand temper chocolate, and dip truffles. They take home about 40 truffles at the end of class.

Saratoga Chocolates offers over 30 different ganache and caramel based bonbons. The dark chocolate confections use a 71% dark chocolate blend. There are also handmade chocolate bars, dipped dried fruits, chocolate sauces, and drinking chocolate mixes. Some of the most popular flavors are Valencia Orange, Coconut Caramel, Chili Spiced, Strawberry Balsamic, Earl Grey, and Grapefruit Honey.

Where to buy: At the retail shop in Sartoga, Online at www.saratogachocolates.com, SF Chocolate Factory, Hotel Los Gatos, Cava Wine Bar, and Beautiful Wishes.

Gateau et Ganache

PO Box 61223 Palo Alto CA 94306 650-384-0859
www.gateauetganache.com

You might be tempted to try to live on a 100% G&G diet for good reason! Gateau et Ganache offers sophisticated, handcrafted confections and chocolates created in the French style. They focus on seasonality, combining the best of local ingredients -- such as organic fruits and cream -- with the finest imported chocolate, liqueurs, and spices.

Gateau et Ganache owner Anni Golding believes in indulging your passion (hence the tag line: Indulge Your Passion!). Of course this refers to a passion for chocolate, but it also extends to passion for enjoyment in food, work, and life. (And for Anni, it's about indulging her passion for creating delicious treats that people enjoy and share with each other.) The fresh, delicious indulgences include: chocolate bonbons & truffles, specialty marshmallows, and seasonal treats, such as Brownies a l'Americaine (fudgy brownies topped with a layer of ganache and a hand-painted chocolate tile).

The bonbon collection changes seasonally, with some flavors available only during certain times of the year, respecting the seasons by incorporating herbs and fruits that are locally and organically produced. For example, the L'Orange Sanguine bonbon is available only during the spring when blood oranges are in season. The Verveine Citronelle (lemon verbena with white chocolate) is only available May to October. The most popular products are: Handmade Chocolate-Dipped Chocolate Marshmallows, French-style bonbons in a variety of flavors, and Les Truffes Classiques (classic dark chocolate truffles). The Chocolate-Dipped Chocolate Marshmallows have the pillowy softness of a marshmallow, combined with the rich flavor of chocolate, and then finished with crisp, thin layer of tempered chocolate.

Says Anni: One of the great things about this business is that our products are part of happy experiences -- the times when people want to share, show gratitude, or celebrate. Gateau et Ganache was started as a specialty cake business, with confections as an afterthought. While developing the cake business, we offered our first selection of bonbons and marshmallows for Valentine's Day in 2005. To our (pleasant) surprise, the chocolates and marshmallows were a hit, so we decided to focus on these products, rather than specialty cakes.

Where to buy: Primary sales are direct, through the website

Gâteau et Ganache

FINE CAKES & CHOCOLATES

LES TRUFFES CLASSIQUES

PALO ALTO, CALIFORNIA

Wine Country Chocolates

14301 Arnold Drive   Glen Ellen   CA   95442   707-996-1010
www.winecountrychocolates.com

Wine Country Chocolates specializes in world class truffles, and is most popular for its wine infused truffles. Because its roots are in the California Wine Country, the theme of the chocolate and of the tasting room are greatly influenced by wine and the surrounding wineries.

The chocolatiers of Wine Country Chocolates are a mother-daughter team; Betty and Caroline Kelly. Caroline is only 21 years old, but already displays the talent of chocolatiers twice her age. The staff of Wine Country Chocolates is like one big family, as many employees have known one another since childhood.

The chocolates are made without the use of preservatives, waxes, or other additives. Everything is made by hand, on-site at the chocolate shop in Glen Ellen. Wine Country Chocolates' truffles maintain a unique creaminess; instead of rolling the truffles they are pressed, in one-of-a-kind dies, and then enrobed in a layer of dark chocolate.

Popular choices are the wine infused truffles, the cappuccino-tiramisu truffle, and the irresistible caramel rocky road. The ambiance of Wine Country Chocolates shop is similar to a typical wine tasting room. They emphasize the Wine Country atmosphere by inviting guests to taste products and sample different percentages of cacao. The shop also gives visitors the opportunity to meet the chocolatiers and watch them create chocolate confections in a viewable kitchen.

Wine Country Chocolates story: You shouldn't eat Wine Country Chocolates while driving! One of our customers first tried our Fresh Orange truffle on his way home. He told us that the truffle was so incredible that he had to pull his car over because he could no longer concentrate on his driving!

Where to buy: You can purchase them at their retail shop in Glen Ellen, or at the following wineries: Ravenswood, Valley of the Moon, Wellington Vineyards, and BR Cohn Winery.

Wine Country Chocolates

The TeaRoom

110-C Mezzetta Court   American Canyon CA 94503 707-561-7080
www.thetearoom.biz

The TeaRoom is a delicious find for chocolate consumers and for businesses, and just one mouthful of its offerings is never enough. In addition to making fine chocolate influenced by tea flavors, the TeaRoom provides chocolate and tea services to Hotel and Promotional enterprises.

Lead by Heinz Rimann, The TeaRoom's hand-crafted, organic, and tea-infused chocolate truffles are created without preservatives. They are also all made on-site with organic Belgian chocolate.

At the San Francisco International Chocolate Salon, the TeaRoom won awards and was swamped by attendees.

Apparently that's not unusual. Says Rimann: At the Expo West Natural Food show in Anaheim, a woman was eating our cocoa-dusted truffle and a woman whispered in her ear (causing her to drop the truffle). We asked her what she said and she replied: "This is culinary orgasm"!

Where to buy: Various hotels as premiums and gift shop items. Amazon and Yahoo ecommerce sites.

Coco-luxe Confections

200 Gate 5 Road #107   Sausalito   CA   94965   415-367-4012
www.coco-luxe.com

Chocolate luxury from stylish founder and choco-latier Stephanie Marcon! Coco-luxe is a confection company that produces gourmet all-natural confections based on fun, familiar flavors. The truffle flavors are based on classic tastes and uniquely identified by playful designs on top of each piece. Coco-luxe also makes dragee nuts and chocolate bars, and its most popular selection is their 9 piece dessert box (pink), and block party almonds.

As you can see from the photographs on these pages, the Coco-luxe packaging and presentation is as outstanding as the Coco-luxe flavors. The style is "retro-whimsical 1960's with a modern twist." It almost merits a place as a collectors item, if it could last that long in storage...or on your display table without being eaten.

Where to buy: Bittersweet Cafe (San Francisco and Oakland), Chocolate Haven (San Francisco), The Candy Store (San Francisco on Polk Street), Andronico's Markets, Bi-Rite (San Francisco), and various other markets in Northern California as well as online and wholesale.

Coco·luxe
CONFECTIONS

DARK CHOCOLATE BAR
WITH CRYSTALIZED
GINGER AND FORTUNE
COOKIE PIECES
NET WT 2.5 oz (70g)

GOOD FORTUNE

Coco·luxe
CONFECTIONS

Coco·luxe
CONFECTIONS

Coco·luxe
CONFECTIONS

Coco·luxe
CONFECTIONS

Block Party
Almonds

cinnamon candied almonds in dark chocolate

NET WT 4.5 oz (128g)

NEWTREE

LAVENDER
Lavande

TRANQUILITY

SOOTHING/APAISANT

FINE BELGIAN MILK CHOCOLATE
FIN CHOCOLAT BELGE AU LAIT

MILK
CHOCOLATE

NEWTREE
Gourmet
Belgian
Chocolate

San Anselmo,
California

Sacred Chocolate

1925 E. Francisco Blvd. # 5   San Rafael   CA   94901   415-342-0527
www.SacredChocolate.com

We pray that Manna from Heaven actually materializes in the chocolate...hence Sacred Chocolate.

Sometimes it's better to hear the story directly from a true believer. In this case, Sacred Chocolate's Steve Adler describes first-hand the Sacred Chocolate power:

"Our chocolate is RAW and never heated above 114 degrees F from bean to bar. We are the manufacturer of a special kind of certified organic chocolate bar that is made with maple sugar and is also certified vegan, Kosher, and Halal. The most special thing about our bars is we only use RAW cacao and the low temperature process takes 5 days to complete and is electronically temperature controlled. As a result, our Ginger recipe for example boasts an impressive 34,000 on the ORAC scale for 100 grams (Blueberries is only about 5000 as a comparison). ORAC is the scale for antioxidant measurement. Furthermore, our

chocolate has next to ZERO trans fatty acids as a result of our special process. Our cacao comes from Ecuador and the farmers are paid above fair trade standards."

Some of the most popular Sacred Chocolate products are Ginger, Mint. Vegan Milk, Jungle Peanut, Amazonian and Pacific Paradise Celebrities that have tasted Sacred Chocolate are Patrick Flanagan, David Wolfe, Gabriel Cousens, and Peter Nigaard.

Where to buy:www. SacredChocolate.com, www.NatuRAW.com, www.Sunfood.com

Sacred Chocolate
San Rafael, California

The Xocolate Bar

248 Laurel Place   San Rafael   CA   94901   415-233-0760
www.TheXocolateBar.com

The Xocolate Bar, founded by Malena Lopez-Maggi and Clive Brown, specializes in beautifully hand-lustered bonbons with exotic flavors like Tamarind-Mango, Lavender-Walnut, and Chile-Orange-Cinnamon. Most of their chocolates have 70% cacao content and all of them contain all-natural, organic and fair-trade ingredients whenever possible. Many of their bonbons are also vegan, but you wouldn't know it by the taste. Because they are both jewelers and artists who enjoy making beautiful things with their hands, Lopez-Maggi and Brown are known for their genius for creativity, as seen in their product lines that include Chakralates (one chocolate for each Chakra), Ganesh Ganache, and Venus of Willendorf figurines. It is no surprise that the most popular items in their collections are the Tamarind-Mango Buddhas, the Vegan Collection, the Lavender Marshmallow Pillows, and the Lavender Walnut Fudge.

Says Malena: The Xocolate Bar (pronounced 'shocolate') gets its name from the Aztec word for chocolate, 'Xocolatl,' because like the Aztecs, we revere chocolate as a food of the gods. All of our chocolates are handmade with love and the finest ingredients available. No artificial flavors and No trans fats. Clive Brown, my life partner and co-chef, is a charming Englishman with a penchant for cardamom and traveling at the drop of a hat. Whether we're in Southeast Asia, Indonesia, South America, or Europe, we always find plenty of inspiration in the cultures and foods that we meet.

Where to buy: Chocolate Covered (San Francisco), San Francisco Chocolate Factory (San Francisco), Artizmo Gallery (Terra Linda, CA), The Potting Shed (Fairfax, CA), and online at www.TheXocolateBar.com.

The Xocolate Bar
San Rafael, California

Couture Chocolates by Ginger Elizabeth
Sacramento, California

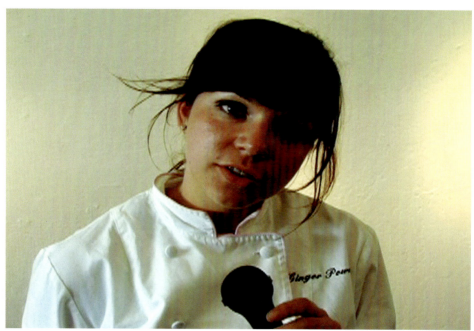

Grand Avenue Chocolates
Concord, California

Images courtesy of the San Francisco International Chocolate Salon

Alegio Chocolate
Berkeley, California

Cosmic Chocolate

5002 Telegraph Ave. Suite B   Oakland   CA   94609   877-612-2639
www.cosmicchocolate.com

An infectious creation from an infectious personality. Founded by Carly Baumann, Cosmic Chocolate's open chocolate mantra is "With a new day rising and a cosmic journey ahead, we invite you to join us towards an explosive affair of the senses." Her Cosmic Bombs, cocktail infused truffles, create luscious bites of elation.

The product is both eye-catching and full of flavor, and matches the vivacity of its creator, Carly. The shape and design of Cosmic Chocolate is influenced by images and graphics that correspond with each collection. Color is a notable part of their creations and they make sure to emphasize the energy and hipness of the product through brilliant arrays. Other products in the line include Cosmic Bliss (heart warming chocolate hearts) and Shangrila Spa truffles.

Cosmic Chocolate's growth in the market has been fantastic. Says Carly of her product release: During our launch, we were called by the Today Show to send samples of our product. Our product was tasted and selected as one of the best chocolates of 2006. The day before the story and our product was to air, I received a phone call requiring 5 more

boxes of our chocolate for display. I was 15 blocks from the Today Show studio and tried desperately to catch a cab. Every cab was full and I resorted to riding in a horse carriage up 5th avenue during rush hour to the Today Show. It was freezing, frenetic, and fabulous; well worth it!!! Plus, Al Roker ate our tequila coke truffle on the Today Show.

Where to buy: At the Cosmic Chocolate location, Whole Foods, the Cosmic website.

Coco Delice Fine Chocolates

P.O. Box 194243   San Francisco   CA   94119-4243   415-407-8413
www.cocodelice.com

Coco Delice's charming owner and master chocolatier Dennis Kearney specializes in dark chocolate confections with a European influence. Chocolates are made with a French influence in both flavor and appearance: darker and less sweet than many other chocolates and possessing an intensity in flavor without being overwhelming in portions. Coco Delice chocolates are produced by hand, in small quantities, using organic cream and only the highest-quality and freshest ingredients, relying on local suppliers to the greatest extent possible.

Popular Coco Delice products include hand rolled Cognac truffles and Caramelized chocolate covered almonds, and flavors such as Salty Caramel, Lavender and Meade Wine, Sonoma Merlot, and Framboise.

Kearney strives to provide the highest quality chocolate experience while balancing business with the environmental issues. Coco Delice does not use excess packaging, boxes are made in California vs. overseas, they use organic ingredients to the extent possible and plan to incorporate fair trade chocolate into the line.

Says Kearney: Our chocolates are elegant but understated. This influence comes from time that I spent in Florence Italy, studying art and noticing that many of the buildings in the city seemed to be understated from the outside. However, when one entered the interior of the these buildings, the real beauty became apparent-intricate carvings, gold leaf, beautiful art, etc. That is the experience I try to create for people.

Where to by: Products can be purchased online through the online boutique, as well as high end retailers such as Whole Foods, The Pasta Shops, Draeger's and GUMP's.

Charles Chocolates

by Anita Chu
Food Writer, Dessert First
dessertfirst.typepad.com

If, like legions of chocoholics everywhere, you thought Willy Wonka's chocolate factory one of the most marvelous places ever dreamed up, you ought to know that a real-life version exists: Charles Chocolates' retail store and candy kitchen in Emeryville.

Charles Siegel, president and CEO of Charles Chocolates, is himself as charming, affable, and devoted to chocolate as Roald Dahl's beloved candy maker. As Siegel shows off the candy kitchen, he expresses his hope that this place will help illuminate the chocolate-making process for the public.

"I really want customers to see what goes into the process of making our chocolates, to understand what we mean when we say everything is made by hand," says Siegel. All of his chocolates are handmade by his workers in small batches - there is no huge warehouse full of candy since everything is made to order and shipped out within a few days. Looking through the soaring glass windows into the kitchen, one can see white-clad workers making blood orange marmalade on the stove, pouring hot caramel into frames to be cut later with a guitar, or wrapping chocolate bars individually in foil. Everything is clean, efficient, and precise - just as Siegel likes it.

Siegel has several pastry chefs overseeing production in his kitchen, all of them with extensive backgrounds in the food industry. Siegel himself is a fixture of the Bay Area chocolate scene; having started his first chocolate company, Attivo Confections, 25 years ago, he served as a consultant for several other chocolate companies before the lure of making his own chocolate made him set up shop once again. His expertise and experience serve him well; there is a surety and focus to his work.

"Chocolate is all about pleasure", Siegel says, and all his chocolates are created around this principle. His classic collection of chocolates includes plump chocolate hearts filled with ganaches of raspberry and passionfruit, luxurious chocolate caramels, elegant truffles flavored with Kahlua and lavender and honey, and adorable butterflies filled with peanut praline. He uses a mix of chocolates from El Rey, Guittard and Cacao Barry to get the right nuances of cacao to match the filling. A must-try is the mojito heart, which has a filling of mint and lime ganache splashed with rum – as close to the real drink as possible.

The most exotic product is a collection of tea-infused chocolates made with some eastern teas from Teance Fine Teas of Berkeley. The collection contains some very unique tasting chocolates that range from delicate (jasmine) to earthy (oolong). Siegel explains that each tea is paired with a different blend of chocolates to achieve a perfect harmony in taste. The lichee and osmanthus chocolates are a particular delight, satisfying smooth squares adorned with calligraphic characters that melt in the mouth into floral, complex richness.

One of Charles Chocolates' signature items – the colorful edible chocolate boxes containing more chocolates inside - was actually born out of necessity. At one point his supplier was unable to deliver enough packaging for Siegel and his chocolates, so he decided to make his own boxes out of chocolate. This brainstorm has turned into a trademark - new designs for new collections are constantly coming out, from a Chinese watercolor-inspired lid for the tea chocolates to a pretty floral pastel for the spring collection.

Siegel doesn't just make great chocolates - he also makes some stellar pate de fruit. His wine infused versions of this French candy are swoon-worthy; they taste like perfect distillations of the grape. Siegel uses wines from Artesa Winery in Napa to make his little hemispheres of bliss - the gewurztraminer and champagne flavors are light and sweet, the merlot and cabernet sauvignon delectably intense.

Charles Chocolates retail store is a sleek little space, with boxes of chocolates seeming to hover on glass shelves backed

and ice cream. "We really want to make this place into a destination spot," Siegel says. He has created a guided tour of the kitchen to satiate the public's quest for knowledge of the chocolate making process and offers the place for private tasting events. His generosity of spirit and infectious enthusiasm are certainly reflected in his store, which stands as a temple to chocolate in its myriad delicious permutations. It is a fantastic addition to the Bay Area's long tradition of local chocolate, and a chance to feel like wide-eyed Charlie Bucket in a sweet, wondrous fantasyland.

Charles Chocolates
Emeryville, CA
www.charleschocolates.com

by art-gallery-chic brick walls. Dominating the center of the room is the candy case, where all of Siegel's confections are artfully displayed and ready to be snapped up by the piece or in a box. Just around the corner is the seating area before the kitchen; customers can relax with a coffee and piece of chocolate and watch workers industriously making more candy. There is a hypnotic pull to seeing workers stirring a huge pot of fleur de sel-flecked caramel or operating the enrobing machine that covers each piece of candy in a perfect embrace of tempered chocolate. It also creates a connection between chocolate and consumer: this is no piece of mass-produced sugary fluff but a confection made just yards away, with an ephemeral shelf life, meant to be savored while it is fresh and new.

Furthering its café aspirations, Charles Chocolates also serves its own house hot chocolate alongside Blue Bottle coffee, and offers homemade pastries

Charles Chocolates

6529 Hollis Street   Emeryville   CA   94608   888.652.4412
www.charleschocolates.com

Charles Chocolates is a culinary phenomenon. In less than 4 years, founder Charles Siegel has created wave after wave of artisan delights. Chuck (Charles) Siegel founded the company three years ago, but has been in the confectionary business for over two decades. Completely self taught, Chuck has set out to bring high quality chocolates to a wide audience, and have a good time in the process. At Charles Chocolates, he expands the concept of premium chocolate confections by using organic herbs, fruits and nuts. Everything is made by hand in very small batches using traditional techniques, and confections are shipped to customers within days of being created.

Charles' product line ranges well over 30 individual confections, such as chocolate bars, orange twigs and caramel almond sticks, and edible chocolate boxes. The most popular items are the triple chocolate almonds, car-amel almond sticks, peanut butterflies and Fleur de Sel caramels.

In 2007 the company opened the Charles Chocolates Store & Chocolate Bar. Inside of its sleek modern interior the Retail Store, Factory and Chocolate Bar are all connected to create an immersive chocolate experience. Through large bay windows, customers may watch the chocolates being made during tours as well as anytime that the Chocolate Bar is open.

Says a spokesperson: One of our signature products is our entirely edible chocolate box. This box has a bittersweet chocolate base and either a white chocolate or milk chocolate lid. We offer several different assortments in the edible chocolate box, each containing a special selection of our handmade confections. Often customers say that eating the edible box and lid was just as fun and delicious as eating the chocolates inside.

Where to buy: Available at over 450 retail locations. For a complete list, go to the website.

Bittersweet Chocolate Cafe

by Anita Chu
Food Writer, Dessert First
dessertfirst.typepad.com

Tucked away on a chic stretch of Fillmore Street where you might least expect a paean to unabashed gastronomic indulgence is Bittersweet Chocolate Cafe, a rustic little cafe devoted entirely to chocolate in all its myriad and marvelous forms.

From the name, one might know to expect chocolate when one enters, yet visitors still come in with wide eyes and mouths in O's, surprised at how many forms of chocolate greet them. Over 120 varieties of chocolate bars from around the world, representing an entire spectrum of flavor, fill the racks on the walls. Bittersweet is the happy brainchild of chocolate lovers who, unable to find their favorite chocolates in the U.S., decided to create that place. Together, Penelope Finnie and Seneca Klassen opened Bittersweet and filled it with chocolates they had discovered and loved on their travels around the world. They have made it their mission to introduce the public to chocolate life beyond Hershey's, See's, and even Scharffen Berger.

There is a dazzling array of brands and types of bars from all over the globe, from Cluziel to Amedei to Pralus, as well as some wonderful American-made creations like Dagoba and Vosges.

There are super-dark-bitter varieties for the purist, milk and white confections, and most excitingly, a rainbow of "surprise" bars, filled with mixes of nuts, fruit, and other intriguing bits.

Among the store favorites are Dagoba's Xocalatl, a spirited take on the increasingly popular chili-and-chocolate combo: the bar starts with a creamy vanilla and nutmeg overtones and it isn't until you're about to swallow that the spice kicks in - a pleasant parting fillip. There is also Vosges' Goji Bar, which has bits of the hottest new superfood, goji berries, and a dash of Himalyan pink salt embedded in lusciously silky milk chocolate. It tastes smooth, with hints of raspberry and currants, and is utterly addictive. For a pure hit of dark chocolate, Amano's Ocumare is unbeatable – rich and complex with notes of red fruit, and a luxuriant long finish on the palate.

Bittersweet Cafe also offers housemade cookies, truffles and cupcakes, and they serve coffee and chocolate drinks - what's a cafe without drinks? The menu of chocolate-themed drinks is also the work of Klassen, who wanted to the store to encompass the many ways to experience chocolate. All of the drinks are made from special blends of premium chocolates, mixed with spices or infused with tea. The Classic is a big seller - a big cup of hot, dark chocolate with a swirl of milk. Other delectable choices include the Spicy, which mixes hot chocolate with hints of chili and cinnamon, and the refreshing Thai Iced Tea, which combines fragrant jasmine tea with bittersweet chocolate.

Klassen happily answers overwhelmed customers' most common query, "Which bar should I buy?" when he is in the cafe. "I find that the public has been very eager to learn more about chocolate, and that's why we're here – to educate them," Klassen says. The outpour of interest and enthusiasm led Klassen to set up a series of chocolate tasting seminars, held in the café, which are designed to introduce people to the concepts and nuances of tasting fine chocolates.

With its pleasingly homey décor and relaxed ambience, Bittersweet is a little slice of chocolate heaven – the perfect place to discover and enjoy a new favorite chocolate.

Bittersweet Chocolate Café
Oakland, CA / San Francisco, CA

Bittersweet Chocolate Cafe
Oakland / San Francisco

Chocolat boutique
Albany, California

Scharffen Berger
Chocolate Maker

914 Heinz Ave.   Berkeley   CA   94710   800-930-4528
www.scharffenberger.com

Scharffen Berger makes fine artisan chocolates that are known for their focused and traditional techniques, as well as their attention to detail in using a large percentage of cacao in the product. For example, the 41% Cacao Milk chocolate is a dark milk chocolate. Other products include the 62% Cacao Semisweet, the 70% Cacao Bittersweet chocolate, and an 82% Cacao Extra Dark bar. Scharffen Berger loves using as much of the cacao bean as possible, which as we all know increases chocolate's possible health and lifestyle benefits.

Currently the most popular products include 5 gram tasting squares, and 1 oz and 3oz bars, which are all available in variety of flavors and packages.

Scharffen Berger searches the world for the finest cacao beans, roasts them by country of origin in small batches and then carefully blends the beans to create delicious chocolate with complex flavor profiles. Scharffen Berger Chocolate Maker was founded by Robert Steinberg and Robert Steinberg. Using a coffee grinder, mortar and pestle, an electric mixer, and a hair dryer to produce their first chocolate, in Robert's home kitchen in 1996, the two tested nearly 30 varieties of cacao beans for flavor. The first official batch of Scharffen Berger chocolate was made in their South San Francisco factory using vintage European equipment. By 2000 the company had outgrown their initial factory space. The company moved into its 27,000 square foot factory in Berkeley, CA in May, 2001. The classic brick and mortar warehouse facility provides manufacturing space and the cool environment needed for chocolate making, as well as houses a retail store. Free public tours are offered there daily featuring chocolate tastings and a factory walk through.

INTERVIEW:

Scharffen Berger Chocolate Maker

Robert Steinberg

Opened in 1996, Scharffen Berger has led the American renaissance of artisan chocolates. From natural cocoa powder to quality dark chocolates, Scharffen Berger is the ingredient of choice for many of the nation's top pastry chefs. The enterprise began when co-founders John Scharffenberger and Robert Steinberg noted that the U.S. consumer was growing in sophistication and appreciation for products like artisan cheeses, breads, wines and beer. With John's background in winemaking and Robert's apprenticeship at Lyon's famous chocolatier, Bernachon, the duo went from cooking in their home kitchens to running an international operation, factory included. "Factory," of course, is a stretch, considering how many of the chocolates are hand-made in small batches. Following the Bernachon tradition of making chocolate from scratch, Scharffen Berger beans are hand-selected from the finest plantations around the world, including Ghana, Venezuela, Madagascar, and the Caribbean. Back in the U.S., the beans are cleaned, roasted, ground, blended, tempered, and molded. Though American in origin, Scharffen Berger has a true French flair.

Explains Robert:

On my first day at Bernachon, I remember walking into the production facility with a mixture of awe, excitement, gratitude, and almost giddy pleasure. I knew that my experience at Bernachon was likely to be crucial to anything I would do in the future related to chocolate. I also recall looking forward to finding answers to the questions that had arisen from my reading about chocolate during the previous eight months. What makes them worth visiting? Bernachon represents a living link to the history of chocolate. As chocolate production has become increasingly industrialized, small artisans, who not only produce chocolate from the bean, but then go on to use it for their own confections and pastries, have virtually disappeared. Bernachon also embodies the principle of valuing quality over volume.

Scharffen Berger goes from raw beans to finished product, even though it takes more resources and time. This is the only way to guarantee the quality of the raw materials and hence the quality of the chocolate. Good chefs, by way of analogy, like to make their own stocks rather than buying pre-made stock. As another analogy, my favorite French expression is "Beh, Oui," said with a slight grunt. As far as I can tell, it is used to express agreement in a matter of fact way.

THE ESSENCE OF

CHOCOLATE

RECIPES FOR BAKING AND COOKING WITH FINE CHOCOLATE

SCHARFFEN BERGER

JOHN SCHARFFENBERGER AND ROBERT STEINBERG

Chocolate Covered
San Francisco

Joseph Schmidt Confections

914 Heinz Ave.   Berkeley   CA   94710   800-930-4528
www.jsc.com

Joseph Schmidt Confections has been crafting premium truffles from Belgian Chocolate, fresh cream and intense flavors since 1983, and is considered a West Coast pioneer of artisan pieces. All the truffles are hand decorated and seasonal collections are packed in one of a kind hand made gift boxes. Schmidt offers a full line of fresh cream truffles packed in whimsical seasonally themed packages. These premium truffles are available in three sizes and in a wide assortment of flavors including Sea Salt Caramel, Double Latte, English Toffee and Champagne.

Fans are always very happy to know that after over 25 years, Joseph Schmidt is still actively involved in the product development process. His expressiveness and themes in chocolate - Handcrafted, Whimsical and Fun - describe the profile and personality of Schmidt products.

Where to buy: Joseph Schmidt Confections has retail stores at 3489 16th Street, in San Francisco, and at 356 Santana Row, in San Jose. Products can also be found at major department stores and specialty grocers.

LIKE CAB FARE FOR CHOCOLATE
as told by Karletta Moniz
Chocolate Guru

I thought I would walk to my Chocolate Tasting class last Friday night. I wanted the exercise and it was a cool evening. But after about two blocks I realized that this was foolhardy. I would arrive sweating. Not pretty when mascara is involved. What was I trying to prove, anyway? At a stop light I saw an empty cab, mouthed the words <<are you free?>> The cab driver nodded <<yes.>> I jumped in.

Tossing in my canvas bag full of chocolate I said to the cab driver <<Great, now I'll get to my gig in plenty of time>>.

<<So what is your gig>>, he asked.

<<I'm teaching a class on how to taste chocolate tonight at the Cheese School of San Francisco.>>

This usually results in a big pause in the conversation. After all, this is a lot of information to process. A class to learn how to taste chocolate? A school for cheese? <<Only in San Francisco.>> You can imagine most people thinking <<How precious>>. But this was a cabby and cabbies are never at a loss for words.

<<I was listening to this program on NPR a couple months ago about some French chocolate maker and some Italian guy...>>

<<Ah, yes. I bet I know what you are talking about>>, I replied and then told him the story about Amedei of Tuscany chocolate and Valrhona.

<<Yeah. That is the story. They said this Italian guy now made the worlds best chocolate. Have you ever tasted it?>>

<<Sure. In fact, I have some in my bag. Do you want to try a piece?>>

<<Really? You do? Yeah, I will try a piece. Where did you get it?>>

<<At Biondivino on Green Street between Polk and Van Ness. Tell Ceri, the owner, that Karletta sent you.>>

I reached into my wallet for the money to pay for my ride.

<<No,>> he waved away my $20 bill. <<No charge. You have been really pleasant. And thanks for the chocolate.....>>

Only in San Francisco....

The Art of Tasting Chocolate
Chocolate Tasting Classes at Your Location
903 Pine Street, #30,
San Francisco, CA, 94108
415-269-7168
www.TheArtofTastingChocolate.com

Do you love chocolate? Join the Culinary Muse, Karletta Moniz, for one hour devoted to your favorite past time - eating chocolate! In 'The Art of Tasting Chocolate' workshop you will learn the difference between chocolate with a 87% cacao content, a 59% cacao content and what the words Forastero, Criollo and Trinitario relate to. Find out what it means when a chocolate bar reads "single estate" versus "single variety". Best of all you will be able to determine which chocolate you prefer and which chocolates may actually be good for your health.

Karletta Moniz is a San Francisco based Food Consultant, Chef and Writer whose client list includes Disney, Neiman-Marcus, Jamba Juice, Seeds of Change, ABC-TV and more...

XOX Truffles
San Francisco and Oakland

Ghirardelli Chocolate Shops at Ghirardelli Square, San Francisco

colleague (and the man responsible for our impromptu meeting) Chuck Siegel of Charles Chocolates has made his own s'mores on and off for twenty years. Start-up confectioner Laura's Candy is also in the s'mores game, and Lisa Adams's new S'mores cookbook offers pages full of variations. For conservative campers who are willing to sacrifice flavor for a bit of nostalgia, Maine-based wilderness outfitter L.L. Bean sells its own s'mores kit (with standard-issue Hershey bars).

Recchiuti of California's S'mores in New York's Central Park

by Emily Stone

By far, the best offer I got one Memorial Day weekend was from a guy I'd never met before. "What do you say we arrange to meet in Central Park and chat chocolate over Recchiuti s'mores?" he asked in an email. "I'll bring the gear, you bring your palate and we can geek out around our favorite topic." Even better that the guy turned out to be Michael Recchiuti himself.

Michael and Jacky Recchiuti are owners of San Francisco's ten-year-old Recchiuti Confections, where the chocolate bon bons are improvisations on ingredients available at the local farmers' market. Michael is the chocolatier and head taster, in addition to the author (with Fran Gage) of Chocolate Obsession and the darling of every writer on the chocolate beat from Mort

Rosenblum to Chloe Doutre-Roussel. On the morning he called to say he'd made it to New York and was on his way to Manhattan, I was out the door in record time.

There was some technical stuff to sort out first. While Michael wrangled a camp stove from a pastry chef at one of the city's poshest dining rooms, I went on a last-minute errand to buy a digital tape recorder at Radio Shack. We met by the steel globe at Columbus Circle and, just as the Central Park thermometer peaked at 85 degrees, we casually strolled past a crew of firemen leaning on their sparkling red truck and set up our

marshmallow-roasting operation in the Sheep Meadow.

As symbolic of the American summer as Memorial Day barbecues, s'mores are a campfire tradition made by sandwiching a molten marshmallow and a chunk of chocolate between two graham crackers. Recchiuti goes against the norm by using a bain-marie to melt the chocolate (his own six-couverture 85%-cacao blend). "The marshmallows never really melt it perfectly, as far as I'm concerned," he told me. But he left the choice between charred and slowly-cooked marshmallows to me. "Everybody has their own way of toasting the marshmallow," he said, "I don't want to assume...." We talked a bit about travel

and love and politics. I have it all on tape--except for the snippet of conversation that was drowned out by the whooping of a police van, prompting us to pack up and stash our camp stove. Anyway, instead of talking we spent most of our time watching the flame, licking our fingers, and enjoying the weather.

Michael Recchiuti's S'Mores Kit, which includes eight vanilla-bean marshmallows and as many homemade graham crackers in addition to the chocolate, can leave

his San Francisco headquarters and be at your door in a couple of days. Recchiuti's Bay Area

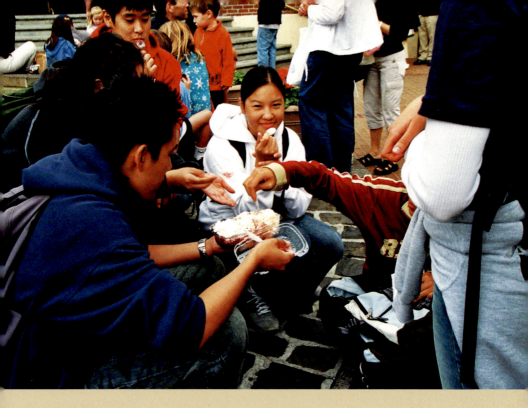

Clockwise from top left (opposite page): A chocolate party, the meeting spot at Fountain Plaza, a Ghirardelli chocolate cafe, Fountain Plaza

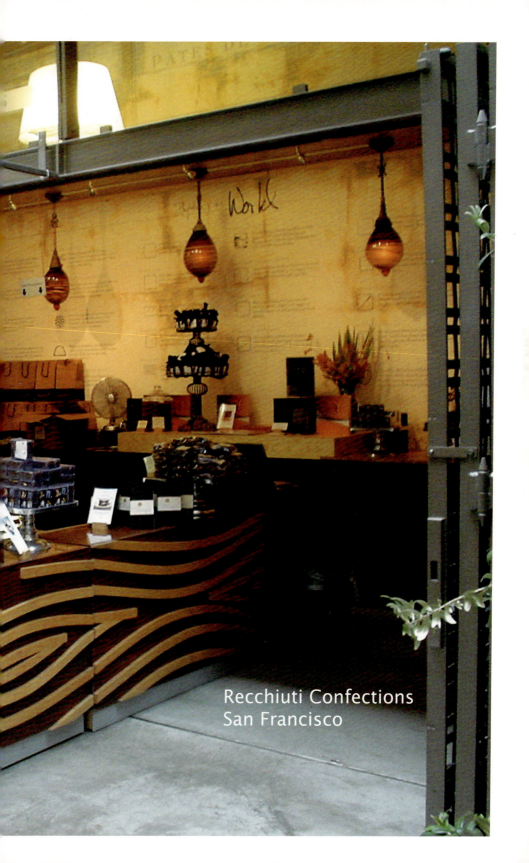

Recchiuti Confections
San Francisco

CHOCOLATE TELEVISION'S
Laurie Gauguin's
San Francisco Chocolate Picks

In a city where nearly every food craving imaginable can be satisfied with its 7-mile radius, we residents of San Francisco have come to expect great things from our food-focused home. Here are my top three chocolate picks in the city.

Cocoa Bella's Exotic Chocolate Collection

With hundreds of international chocolates to choose from at Cocoa Bella, sometimes it's impossible for me to decide what to try. That's when I pick up an Exotic Chocolate Collection—a carefully selected assortment of unusual flavors from Europe and the United States which includes pieces from some of my favorite chocolatiers: Knipschildt, Christopher Elbow and Michel Clu-

izel (among others). I then go home and play the "eeny-meeny-miney-moe" game, knowing that every choice will be a winner.

Bittersweet Café's classic hot chocolate with a homemade spiced marshmallow

There's no better way to shake off the blustery San Francisco weather than with a cup of Bittersweet's hot chocolate. My choice is The Classic—a decadent blend of dark chocolate and milk that's rich enough to fulfill my most intense chocolate craving. For added indulgence, I top my cup with a homemade spiced marshmallow that's big enough to last through the final sip without melting away to nothing.

Recchiuti Confections' dark milk chocolate bar

High-percentage dark chocolates are all the rage, but sometimes all I want is a soothing bite of milk chocolate. Recchiuti's 55% dark milk chocolate bar is wonderfully creamy from start to finish, not too sweet, and has delicious hints of caramel that echo the flavors I loved as a kid, only better.

CHILE-SPIKED CINNAMON BROWNIES

Mild ancho chiles and cinnamon give these fudgy brownies a spicy kick. For best results, use Ceylon cinnamon for its light and fruity flavor.

1. Preheat oven to 325° F. Cut the butter into cubes, then put it and the chocolate into a medium metal mixing bowl. Set the bowl over simmering water, stirring occasionally, until melted. Remove bowl from the heat and set it aside until the chocolate mixture is warm, but not hot, about 20 minutes.

2. Meanwhile, tear the chile in half, remove all of the seeds, then tear the flesh into a few pieces. Pour boiling water over the chile pieces, then set aside until softened, about 5 minutes.

3. Drain and chop the chiles. In a small saucepan, heat 2 table-spoons of sugar with 1 tablespoon of water, stirring until the sugar is melted. Add the chiles and cook over low heat, stirring constantly, until most of the liquid evaporates. Scrape the candied chiles into a glass or ceramic bowl. Cool completely.

4. In a small bowl, mix together the remaining 1 cup and 2 tablespoons of sugar, cocoa, cinnamon and salt. Add the sugar mixture to the cooled chocolate mixture, mixing well, then stir in the candied chiles. Whisk in the eggs, then add the flour and mix just until smooth (do not overmix).

5. Line an 8" x 8" glass baking pan with aluminum foil. Pour the brownie batter into the pan, smoothing the top with a damp spatula. Bake on the center rack at 325° F for 30 to 40 minutes, until a toothpick inserted into the center of the brownies comes out almost clean. Cool brownies completely, then invert the pan onto a cutting board. Remove the aluminum foil, trim the brownie edges, then cut into 16 squares.

Yield: 16 brownies

3 oz. (6 Tbs.) butter

4 oz. unsweetened baking chocolate

1 large dried ancho chile, about 6 inches long

1 cups sugar, divided

1 Tbs. non-alkalized unsweetened cocoa, sifted

1 tsp. cinnamon, preferably Ceylon

1 tsp. salt

2 large eggs, lightly beaten

1 cup flour

Recipe courtesy of chef/writer Laurie Gauguin.

How to Interview a Chocolatier and Taste Their Chocolate for CHOCOLATE TELEVISION

Laurie Gauguin
Host, TasteTV

Step 1: Introduce the chocolatier to the television audience

Step 2: Listen carefully to the processes, themes and ingredients that distinguish this chocolate from others.

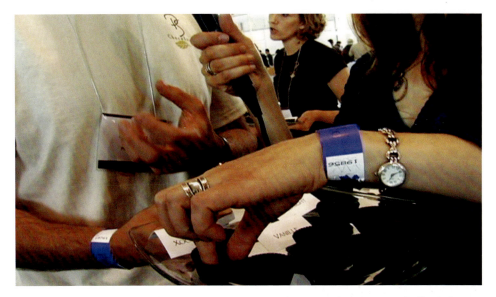

Step 3: Accept the offer to taste the chocolate, and then carefully select the most appealing piece

Step 4: Carefully place the chocolate on your tongue

Step 5: Savor the flavors, textures, and workmanship while trying to identify key ingredients and notes.

Step 6: Tell us what you have experienced in a way that makes us feel as if we have tasted (or want to taste) the same piece.

Note: Try to avoid terms like, "Wow, that tasted great."
We already know it did, but what did it actually taste like?

For more from Chocolate Taster Laurie Gauguin,

see Laurie's Blog, ladleandwhisk.wordpress.com

Ladle and Whisk
Blogging by an industry professional

More of the lovelies

Posted October 4th, 2007 by Laurie

Categories: Miscellaneous, Uncategorized

Comments: Be the first to comment

Is there anything more perfect?

Posted October 4th, 2007 by Laurie

ABOUT LAURIE

Laurie has cooked and baked professionally since 1996. She currently works in San Francisco as a private chef, tasting panel member, recipe developer and writer.

October 2007

S	M	T	W	T	F	S
	1	2	3	4	5	6
7	8	9	10	11	12	13
14	15	16	17	18	19	20
21	22	23	24	25	26	27
28	29	30	31			

« Sep

Search

Good Reads/Views

101 Cookbooks
Becks and Posh
Between Meals
chez pim
Chocolate and Zucchini
Chowhound
David Lebovitz

for the palate, they are al~
sustainable harvested, and promote a better i
for farming families.

USDA Organic & Fair Trade Certified™.

>> 100% recyclable packaging, prin
 based inks

Oreg ilth.

The San Francisco Chocolate Factory
San Francisco, California

Images courtesy of the San Francisco International Chocolate Salon

Poco Dolce, San Francisco, California

Opposite Page: Poco Dolce assortment and toffee.

This page: Poco Dolce's signature salt enhances the flavor of chocolate.

Images from the San Francisco International Chocolate Salon

Cocoa Bella Chocolates
San Francisco, California

Trader Joe's Chocolates

Images courtesy of the San Francisco International Chocolate Salon

Chocoholics Divine Desserts

18819 Highway 88   Clements   CA   95227   800-760-CHOC
www.gourmetchocolate.com

Sexy is the right word for this chocolate. Chocoholics Divine Desserts is a chocolate manufacturer that offers premium chocolates, signature sauces and adult novelty items, including romance-and-chocolate themed games.

One can only assume that their most busy seasons are Valentine's, Xmas, birthdays, weddings, anniversaries, third dates, and... probably most of the time.

Their chocolate sauces are also useful for many indoor activities, but we have found them to be perfect for making chocolate waffles in the morning (or evening, depending on "client" demand).

The retail store is in an award winning building and listed in the National Register of historic places,

and the factory is an AIA award winner with an observation hall that runs the length of the building . This hall allows visitors to view the fascinating world of chocolate making and gift packaging. They also have Monthly Wine Tastings, where they invite local wineries into the retail store and host a wine tasting.

Chocoholics appears in many boutiques and gourmet stores, and gets media coverage on outlets such as the Travel Channel, Food Network, Good Morning America, CNN Early Edition, KCRA, NBC, Fox, and the Late Late Show .

Where to buy: Products are available on the website and in stores nationwide.

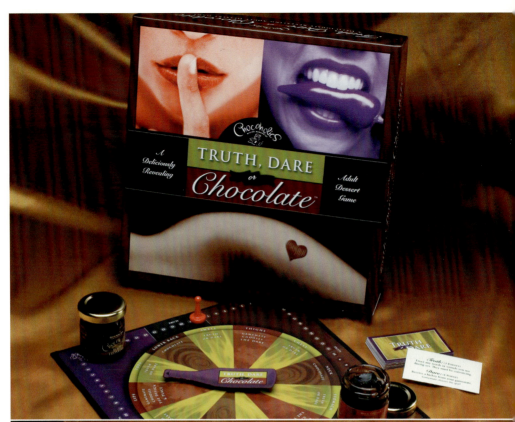

Chocoholics Divine Desserts
Clements, California

Chocoholics Divine Desserts
Clements, California

SAN FRANCISCO'S BEST CUPCAKES: 2008 PICKS

Culinary lifestyle media exec A.K. Crump says if you can't eat birthday cake every day, go for the next best thing. Plus, chocolate is a staple flavor. Here's his list of the best this year to get your cupcake fix.

1. Karas Cupcakes set a new standard for gourmet cupcakes when it opened. It is now not unusual to see their cupcakes being served in place of birthday or even wedding cakes. Teary-eyed customers stand at the counters, patiently awaiting bliss.

Flavor combinations include:
Vanilla cupcake with passion fruit filling and vanilla buttercream,
Meyer Lemon vanilla cupcake with a tart lemon filling and lemon buttercream,
Banana Caramel banana cupcake with caramel filling and silky cream cheese frosting
and
Fleur Del Sel chocolate cupcake with caramel filling, ganache frosting& fleur del sel

Wow!

3249 Scott Street (at Chestnut), San Francisco, California, P 415 563-CAKE
Ghirardelli Square, Plaza Level, 900 North Point, San Francisco, California

2. Noe Valley Bakery is always creating new cupcakes based on season or holiday.
4073 24th St. at Castro   (415) 550-1405

3. Citizen Cake just can't be beat. The regular cupcakes have vanilla beans. The fancy ones are hard to describe.
399 Grove St   (415) 861-2228

4. Destination Bakery in Glen Park is truly a worthwhile destination. Fresh butter cream frosting on everything.
598 Chenery St,   (415) 469-0730

5. Blissful Bites is new to the scene, but the husband has culinary credentials, and the cupcakes are addictive.
397 Arguello, (415) 750-9460

Windsor Confections
4632 Telegraph Avenue
Oakland, CA 94609
www.windsorconfections.com

Grand Avenue Chocolates
1021 Detroit Ave.
Concord, CA 94518
877.934.180
www.grandavenuechocolates.com

Sweet Sweet Confections
P.O. Box 6184
San Jose, CA 95150-6184
888.878.2941
www.sweetsweetconfections.com

Cocoa Bon
Los Gatos, CA
www.cocoabon.com

All photographs courtesy of each company listed above

Holy Chocolate . Mar Toma Enterprise
1420 W. Latimer Ave #5
Campbell, CA 95008
408.374.0531
www.holychocolate.com

The San Francisco Chocolate Factory
286 12th Street
San Francisco, CA 94103
888.732.4626
www.sfchocolate.com

Cacao Anasa Chocolates
P.O. Box 210538
San Francisco, CA 94121
415.846.9240
www.cacaoanasa.com

Annettes Chocolates Factory
1321 First Street
Napa, CA 94559
707.252.4228
www.annettes.com

Woodhouse Chocolate
1367 Main Street
St. Helena, CA 94574
800.966.3468
www.woodhousechocolate.com

All photographs courtesy of each company listed above

Monterey Bay Chocolates
1291 Fremont Blvd
Seaside
CA
(831) 899-7963

Chocolate Dream Box
710 Blossom Hill Dr
Los Gatos
CA

Aida Opera Candies
1375 Burlingame Ave Ste 104
Burlingame
CA
(650) 344-3333

California Candy Co
1204 Burlingame Ave Ste 6
Burlingame
CA

Guittard Chocolate Co
10 Guittard Rd
Burlingame
CA

Nuts For Candy
1241 Broadway
Burlingame
CA

Simply Delicious Sweets
80 Cabrillo Hwy N
Half Moon Bay
CA

See's Candies
(4844 El Camino Real
Los Altos
CA

Charlotte's Confections
1395 El Camino Real
Millbrae
CA

The Chocolate Tree
197 Nevada Street
Redwood City
CA
650-261-9118

Beard Papa's Cream Puffs
835 Middlefield Road
Redwood City
CA
(650) 365-7272

Kelly's Coffee & Fudge
Factory
1150 El Camino Real
San Bruno
CA
(650) 877-9250

Chocolate Mousse Bakery
617 Laurel Street
San Carlos
CA
(650) 593-1966

Miette Confiserie
449 Octavia St
San Francisco
CA

See's Candies
350 Powell Street
San Francisco
CA
(415) 434-4013

Cocoa Bella Chocolates
845 Market St Ste 161
San Francisco
CA

Edible Arrangements
669 Townsend St
San Francisco
CA

Godiva Chocolatier
865 Market Street
San Francisco
CA
(415) 543-8910

Naturally Edible
50 Post St Ste 44
San Francisco
CA

Confetti Le Chocolatier
525 Market Street
San Francisco
CA
(415) 543-2885

Recchiuti Confections
1 Ferry Building Ste 30
San Francisco
CA

Scharffen Berger
Chocolate Maker
1 Ferry Building
San Francisco
CA

Sterling Truffle Bars
480 2nd St
San Francisco
CA

Munchies Paradise
905 Grant Ave
San Francisco
CA

Neuhaus Chocolatier
170 O Farrell Street
San Francisco
CA
(415) 834-1668

Sweet Mart
727 Washington St
San Francisco
CA

Teuscher Chocolate
307 Sutter Street
San Francisco
CA
(415) 834-0850

Richart Chocolate
393 Sutter St
San Francisco
CA
415-291-9600

Schmidt Joseph Confections
2000 Folsom St
San Francisco
CA

Confetti Le Chocolatier
100 Drumm St
San Francisco
CA
(415) 362-1706

Godiva Chocolatier
2 Embarcadero Ctr Ste 2
San Francisco
CA

Belgano
3901 24th Street
San Francisco
CA
(415) 647-4266

Chocolate Covered
4069 24th Street
San Francisco
CA
(415) 641-8123

Chocolate on Castro
504 Castro St
San Francisco
CA

Joseph Schmidt Confections
3489 16th St
San Francisco
CA

Chocolate Covered
4069 24TH St
San Francisco
CA

Five Star Truffles and Coffee
411 Divisadero St
San Francisco
CA
(415) 552-5128

Edible Arrangements
2675 Geary Blvd #203C
San Francisco
CA

Sweet House
3512 Balboa St
San Francisco
CA

Cocoa Bella Chocolates
2102 Union St
San Francisco
CA

Goldleaf Chocolatier
2250 Union St
San Francisco
CA

LUV BOX Chocolates
2078 Chestnut St
San Francisco
CA
(415) 441-1177

Moonstruck Chocolate Cafe
2109 Chestnut St
San Francisco
CA

Shaw's of San Francisco
122 West Portal Avenue
San Francisco
CA
415.681.2702

Godiva Chocolatier
3251 20th Avenue
San Francisco
CA
(415) 566-5058

Chocolat
2801 Leavenworth St
San Francisco
CA

Rainbow Chocolates Forever
31 Medau Pl
San Francisco
CA

Rocky Mountain Chocolate
Factory
65 Jefferson Street
San Francisco
CA
(415) 982-0611

San Francisco Chocolate Store
145 Jefferson St
San Francisco
CA

Z Cioccolato
474 Columbus Ave
San Francisco
CA

Chocolate Heaven
39 Pier Ste D1
San Francisco
CA
(415) 421-1789

Fudge House
39 Pier Ste K2
San Francisco
CA

XOX Truffles
754 Columbus Ave
San Francisco
CA

Stella Pastry Cafe
446 Columbus Ave
San Francisco
CA

Satura Cakes
320 University Avenue
Palo Alto
CA
(650) 326-3393

Teuscher Chocolates of
Switzerland
680 Stanford Shopping Center
Palo Alto
CA
(650) 384-0916

Godiva Chocolatier
180 El Camino Real
Palo Alto
CA

Candie Land
365 2nd Ave
San Mateo
CA

Godiva Chocolatier
3400 S El Camino Real Ste 212
San Mateo
CA

Munchie Bees
2321 Santa Clara Ave
Alameda
CA

N K Chocolates
1616 Lafayette St
Alameda
CA

Tinys
1604 Webster St
Alameda
CA

The Chocolate Bear
P.O. Box 1329
Alamo
CA
(707) 746-4860

Gold Rush Kettle Korn LLC
4690 E 2nd St
Benicia
CA

Elaine's Toffee Co
713 Acorn Dr
Clayton
CA

Dulceria Sanchez
1500 Monument Blvd
Concord
CA

Candy Bar
1850 Gateway Blvd
Concord
CA

Candy Elyse
173 Sun Valley Mall
Concord
CA

Mad About Berries
606 Sycamore Valley Rd W
Danville
CA

Annabelle Candy Co
27211 Industrial Blvd
Hayward
CA

Main Street Sweets
815 Main St
Martinez
CA

Truffle Temptations
1410 Camino Peral
Moraga
CA

Vintage Sweet Shoppe
3261 Browns Valley Rd
Napa
CA

Chocowit Candy Co
135 Camino Dorado Ste 9
Napa
CA

Anette's Chocolate Factory
1321 1st Street
Napa
CA
707.252.4228

Rocky Mountain Chocolate Factory
1219 Napa Town Ctr
Napa
CA

Vintage Sweet Shoppe
530 Main St.
Napa
CA

Dulceria Jenny
1636 E 14th St
San Leandro
CA

Loard's Ice Cream & Candies
2000 Wayne Ave
San Leandro
CA

Ghirardelli Soda Fountain and
Chocolate Shop
1111 139th Ave
San Leandro
CA

Sweet Liaison Chocolates
12919 Alcosta Blvd Ste 10B
San Ramon
CA

Blommer Chocolate
1515 Pacific St
Union City
CA
(510) 471-4300

Kerry Sweet Ingredients
33063 Western Ave
Union City
CA

Godiva Chocolatier
1412 Stoneridge Mall Rd
Pleasanton
CA

Sun-Maid Growers
4683 Chabot Dr Ste 100
Pleasanton
CA

Artisians Sweets
1322 Boulevard Way
Walnut Creek
CA

Leonidas Chocolates
1397 N Main St.
Walnut Creek
CA

Moonstruck Chocolate Cafe
1273 Locust St
Walnut Creek
CA

Hershey Co
1470 Maria Ln
Walnut Creek
CA

Dulceria La Rosa
3606 International Blvd
Oakland
CA

Serendipity Chocolates
Incorporated
638 2nd St
Oakland
CA

Godiva Chocolatier
5645 Bay St
Emeryville
CA
(510) 595-0185

Godiva Chocolatier
5645 Bay St
Emeryville
CA

Hooper's Chocolates
4632 Telegraph Ave
Oakland
CA
(510) 653-3703

Michael Mischer Chocolates
3352 Grand Avenue
Oakland
CA
(510) 986-1822

Dancing Bears' Confections
999 Sunnyhills Rd
Oakland
CA

Le Bonbon
2050 Mountain Blvd
Oakland
CA
(510) 339-2962

Le Bonbon
2050 Mountain Blvd
Oakland
CA

Bittersweet Chocolate Cafe
5427 College Avenue
Oakland
CA
(510) 654-7159

Barlovento Chocolates
2320 Jefferson Ave
Berkeley
CA

Lisa Lerner Chocolates
2984 San Pablo Ave
Berkeley
CA

Edible Love Chocolates
2611 Woolsey Street
Berkeley
CA
(415) 505-0786

Alegio Chocolate
1511 Shattuck Ave
Berkeley
CA
(510) 435-3586

California Candy
1876 Euclid Ave
Berkeley
CA

Masse's Pastries
1469 Shattuck Ave
Berkeley
CA

Scharffen Berger Chocolate
914 Heinz Avenue
Berkeley
CA

Barry-Callebaut
125 Larkspur St Ste 214
San Rafael
CA
(415) 458-1617

Marin Chef
627 Del Ganado Road
San Rafael
CA

The Candy Store On Main Street
7 Main Street
Tiburon
CA
(415) 435-0434

Joanne's Sweet Temptations
114 Meernaa Ave
Fairfax
CA

Lyla's Chocolates
417 Miller Ave
Mill Valley
CA

Le Belge Chocolatier
37 Commercial Blvd Ste 108
Novato
CA
(415) 883-6781

Munchies
613 Bridgeway
Sausalito
CA

Buckhart's Candies
115 San Jose Ave
Capitola
CA
(831) 475-1286

Candy Land
205 Capitola Ave
Capitola
CA

Carousel Taffy
115 San Jose Ave
Capitola
CA

Sweet Factory
1855 41st Ave Ste 262
Capitola
CA

Chocolate Dream Box
710 Blossom Hill Dr
Los Gatos
CA

Cool Bean Mints
14125 Capri Dr Ste 3
Los Gatos
CA

Sri Krishna Sweets
1208 S Abel St
Milpitas
CA

Chocolate Affaire
603 E Calaveras Blvd
Milpitas
CA

Viva La Cioccolata
3501 Thomas Rd
Santa Clara
CA

Donnelly Fine Chocolates
1509 Mission St
Santa Cruz
CA

Mackenzies Chocolates
1492 Soquel Avenue
Santa Cruz
CA
(831) 425-1492

Dolphin Natural Chocolates
41 Hangar Way
Watsonville
CA

Joseph Schmidt
356 Santana Row Apt 319
San Jose
CA

Blackforest Chocolates
P.O. box 901
Arnold
CA
209 795-9282

Peter Rabbit's Chocolate
Factory
2489 Guerneville Rd
Santa Rosa
CA
(707) 575-7110

Heart's Desire Chocolate
631 4th St
Santa Rosa
CA
(707) 528-9061

Mendocino Chocolate Company
542 North Main Street
Fort Bragg
CA
(707) 964-8800

La Dolce V Fine Chocolates
110 N. Main St.
Sebastopol
CA
(707) 829-2178

The Chocolate Cow
452 1st St E Ste F
Sonoma
CA
(707) 935-3564

Stu Lambert Incorporated
899 Broadway
Sonoma
CA

THE CHOCOLATE GUIDE TO

NEVADA, UTAH, OREGON, WASHINGTON, AND BRITISH COLUMBIA

Gigantic Chocolate Fountain
Jean Phillippe Patisserie at the Bellagio
Las Vegas, Nevada

This 27-feet tall, glass-enclosed, floor-to-ceiling chocolate fountain circulates
nearly two tons of melted dark, milk and white chocolate at a rate of 120 quarts

per minute. The fountain's six spouts in the ceiling initiate the descent of rich dark, velvety milk and glistening white chocolate streams through a maze of 25 suspended glass vessels. The colored streams and vessels are staggered, creating a mosaic effect in earthy shades of cocoa, gleaming viscous surfaces and refracted light.

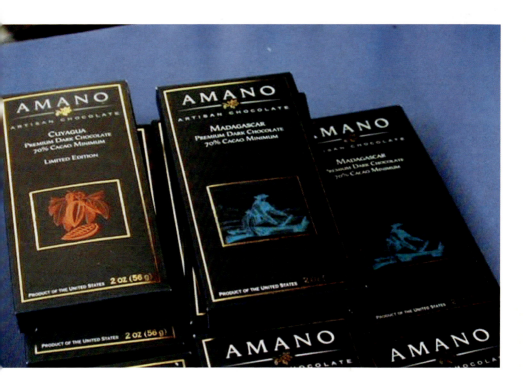

Amano Artisan Chocolate

496 South 1325 West   Orem   Utah   84058   801-655-1996
www.amanochocolate.com

Cofounded by Art Pollard and Clark Goble, Amano is a true luxury product that you can eat every single day (and maybe even feel healthy doing it, since it's so dark, delicious and pure). The founders create what they believe to be some of the world's finest chocolate, and many people agree. The chocolate is made in small batches, using beans first roasted in an antique vintage roaster, then crushed and the husk that surrounds each bean is winnowed away. The bits of bean or "nibs" are then stone ground in a 1930's vintage melangeur, and the sugar is added and the chocolate is refined and finally conched to develop the flavor. Whew, that's a lot of work, but we'll eat the results anytime.

The resulting Amano products won big awards at the 2007 San Francisco International Chocolate Salon, and include: the Ocumare Grand Cru 70% Dark Chocolate Bar - Made solely from beans from the Ocumare valley in Venezuela; the Madagascar Premium 70% Dark Chocolate Bar -- Made solely from beans from the North West coast of Madagascar having a light chocolate flavor but has strong hints of citrus or raspberry; and the Cuyagua Premium 70% Dark Chocolate Bar --

Made solely from beans from the Cuyagua valley in Venezuela. with a rich and complex chocolate flavor with notes of spice.

Amano is influenced by the chocolate makers of Northern Italy and Southern France. In this area, there is a strong chocolate tradition. There are many small chocolate makers that never see much distribution beyond their local area. While there are many "average" chocolate makers, some are great artists in this area and are highly skilled in their craft.

Says Pollard: Not only do we make our own chocolate but we source our ingredients ourselves directly from the farmers or local co-ops.

Where: Premium outlets and the website: www.amanochocolate. com.

Pacific Northwest Chocolate:
The Trip I Didn't Take

By Emily Stone

On a recent weekend I started taking driving lessons--again. My instructor this time around is Helen Gerhardt, a fellow grad student, a former soldier, and an astonishingly generous soul with a little red VW bug. A few more rides around the block with Helen and I'll be able to take on Matt Gross, the New York Times' Frugal Traveler who spent the summer driving cross country.

Gross's travelogue came to an end in the Sunday Times, with the travel writer pulling into Seattle. That Pacific Northwest city was the intended endpoint of my West Coast excursion last summer. But every trip must adjust to its travelers, and Barbara and I chose to stay comfortably within 100 miles of our starting point (and enjoy each other's company) rather than to attempt the (for us, then) impossible feat of traveling eight times that distance across three states.

Lillie Belle Farms, Jacksonville, OR
An indie businessman and a keeper of organic strawberry fields, owner Jeff Shepherd is one of the nicest guys I've met, and the only one who can make the blue-cheese chocolate truffle work.

But if I had made it north from California into Oregon and Washington, these are the chocolate outfits I would have visited, glowing with enthusiasm:

Moonstruck Chocolate, Portland, OR
These confectionery classicists are chocolatiers to the Academy Awards.

Dagoba, Ashland, OR
Frederick Schilling's all-organic chocolate factory (with roots in Costa Rica, the Dominican Republic, Ecuador, Peru, and Madagascar) turns out couverture, flavored bars, and spiritually-infused elixirs.

Sahagún Handmade Chocolates, Portland, OR
Named for Fray Bernardino de Sahagún, the sixteenth-century chronicler of indigenous American society, Elizabeth Montes's fruit and herb (and jalapeno and pumpkin-seed) bon bons are tied to their Aztec heritage.

Emily's Chocolates, Fife, WA
How could I resist?

Fran's Chocolates, Seattle, WA
A Seattle institution, Fran Bigelow is the instigator of the fleur-de-sel caramel craze.

Theo, Seattle, WA
Possibly America's most progressive chocolate maker, one-year-old Theo produces sublime couverture and the "3400 Phinney" collection of flavored bars, including "Coconut Curry Milk Chocolate" and "Bread and Chocolate Dark Chocolate."

Above: Sahagun's shop in Portland.

Left: Emily's Chocolates Chocolate Covered Macadamia Nuts

Below: Theo Chocolate

IMAGES OF
Sahagun's Chocolates in Portland.

For more from Chocolate Lover Emily Stone,

see Emily's Blog, chocolateincontext.blogspot.com

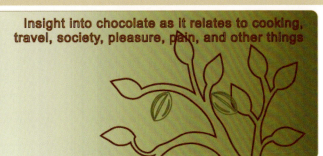

Insight into chocolate as it relates to cooking, travel, society, pleasure, pain, and other things

CHOCOLATEINCONTEXT

SATURDAY, SEPTEMBER 29, 2007

Freelance Chocolate

The month ahead promises to bring harvest festivals, Halloween candy, and (in spite of writer's block, procrastination, and missed deadlines) more of my writing on chocolate in more publications.

My "Vintage Australia" is the cover story of this month's *Budget Travel*. Before I left Terra Australis Incognita last year, I scoured the Yarra Valley, a region recognized more for its wine and its emerging vineyard inns than for its chocolate. Still, I managed to work chocolate maker Kennedy & Wilson (my old standby in Melbourne) into the trip.

I'll also continue to cover chocolate news for Serious Eats in October and beyond. (My latest post highlights the environmentally-sustainable goings-on at Theo Chocolate in Seattle.)

POSTED BY EMILY STONE AT 2:53 P.M.   2 COMMENTS

SATURDAY, SEPTEMBER 22, 2007

EMILY STONE

I'm a chocolate enthusiast. I'm also an itinerant traveler, a lover of literature, and a native New Yorker. I've been a movie reviewer, a reproductive health researcher, and an independent bookstore owner. My writing has appeared in the magazines *Budget Travel*, *Travel + Leisure*, and *Time Out New York*, as well as on the websites World Hum and Epicurious.

Email me!

The Search Begins...

Cary's of Oregon

413 Union Ave.   Grants Pass   OR   97527   888-822-9300
www.carysoforegon.com

Cary's is a maker of premium English Toffee known for "soft-crunch" texture and flavorful combinations. Their gourmet toffee comes in 7 different flavors, including milk chocolate/almond, dark chocolate/ almond, dark chocolate/ espresso, milk chocolate chai, dark chocolate/mango, dark chocolate/hazelnut, and Toffee Fingers. The milk chocolate/almond toffee is their most popular product, with the dark chocolate/ almond being a close second. (Cary's Trail Toffee was a Finalist in the Outstanding Snack category at the prestigious Fancy Food Show.)

The story goes that Cary Cound, founder of the company, had a background in mechanical engineering, but always dreamed of making a business out of an English Toffee recipe his wife's grandfather had given him. He was encouraged by friends and family to do so after they received "toffee" gifts for various occasions. Finally in 2001 he took the big step and opened Cary's of Oregon. His background in mechanical engineering came in handy when different equipment needed to be built or "tweaked" to suit his needs. Today, depending on the season Cary's employs up to 45 people and ships candy all over the country and to Europe.

Cary's toffee is addictive in taste and texture, and this has wide appeal. The Dark Espresso was the snack of the day on national television's Rachael Ray Show. Cary's products are also regularly included in Hollywood goodie and swag bags. Cary's also has an on-site showroom in Oregon, with boxed candies, gift baskets and factory "seconds." There is also a viewing window so visitors can watch the candy being made in the factory.

Where to buy: Available at various retailers throughout the country including Cocoabella, selected Whole Foods Stores, Mollie Stones, Baron's Markets,Metropolitan Markets, etc.

Cary's of Oregon

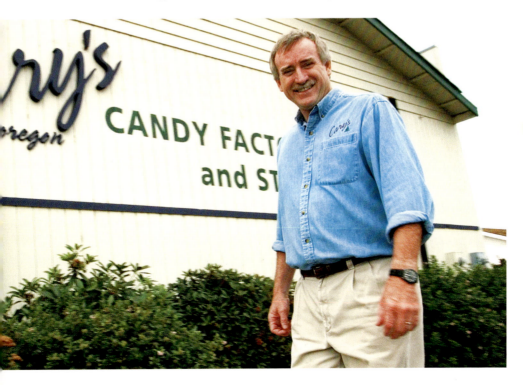

Dagoba Organic Chocolate

1105 Benson Way   Ashland   OR   97520   541-482-2001
dagobachocolate.com

Dagoba Organic Chocolate has taken the chocolate world by storm, offering exceptional chocolate products made with organic and sustainably grown cacao and innovative flavor combinations.

Dagoba was among the first organic chocolate manufacturers in the USA, and was named "Best Dark Chocolate" by the San Francisco Chronicle. The first Dagoba bar was the chai bar, inspired by founder Frederick Schilling's days as a chef at the Naropa Institute. This set the Dagoba signature as a company that provides innovative flavors that are top sellers, such as a their Lavender-Blueberry bar.

Founder Frederick Schilling is passionate about the vision that led him to create this company: creating premium world class chocolate while showing that a socially responsible business can be successful. He has inspired others in the industry to join this approach and remains active as the chief bean sourcer and product developer while working to develop on the ground partnerships that improve cacao quality, expand organic production and support biodiverse reforestation in cacao regions. He views chocolate as a process of alchemy – literally transforming cacao into edible gold. (His guiding force in creation is the "Art of Chocolate Alchemy")

Dagoba follows a comprehensive sustainability framework "Full Circle Sustainability" that ensures the best in quality, ecology, equity and community. Powered by 100% renewable energy, it uses ecologically friendly materials for all packaging, collateral and office/facility needs.

The Dagoba Organic Chocolate tasting room and store feature both photos and detailed illustrations that bring cacao, and the people and environment that surround it, to customers.

Where to buy: Quite a few gourmet and specialty retailers carry Dagoba, fortunately for us, as does their primary sales location on 1105 Benson Way Ashland, Oregon.

DAGOBA
ORGANIC CHOCOLATE
chai
milk chocolate, crystallized ginger and spices
Net. Wt. 2 Oz. 56.7 g   Cacao content: 37%

DAGOBA
ORGANIC CHOCOLATE
seeds
hemp, pumpkin & sunflower seeds
Net. Wt. 2 Oz. 56.7 g   Cacao content

super fruit

lemon~ginger

nibs

DAGOBA
Pacuare 68%
Costa Rican Trinitario

74% cacao

DAGOBA
ORGANIC CHOCOLATE
xocolatl
rich dark chocolate
chilies & nibs

THE ART OF
CHOCOLATE ALCHEMY™
Net. Wt. 2.83 OZ (80 g)

Lillie Belle Farms Hand Made Chocolates, Jacksonville, Oregon

This page: Jeff demonstrates how to paint with chocolate.

Images from the San Francisco International Chocolate Salon

Theo Chocolate

3400 Phinney Avenue North   Seattle   Washington   98103
206-632-5100   www.theochocolate.com

Theo Chocolate has class, style, and presence. In fact, Theo has also helped create a class of its own. Theo is among the first organic and fair trade certified cocoa roasting factories in the United States, and they continue to be a leader in this chocolate product category. Founder Joseph Whinney was is said to be the first person to bring organic cocoa into the United States, and also was tapped to help movie star and entrepreneur Paul

Newman and his daughter, Nell, to source chocolate for the launch of their cookie and candy bar line.

Theo currently has 2 lines of chocolate bars, the 3400 Phinney Chocolate Factory and the Theo Chocolate bars. The 3400 Phinney Chocolate Factory has 3 milk chocolate and 3 dark chocolate bars with flavor inclusions. The Theo Chocolate has 5 origin designated dark chocolate bars. The company also produces a line of ganache filled confections. The bar packaging is richly colored and invokes the cultures of the lands where Theo's cocoa beans are grown.

The Theo factory is set in a beautiful historic building in Seattle where tours of the operation are offered each day.

Where to buy: Whole Foods, most natural food stores, and lots of specialty grocery stores.

theo
chocolate

340
PHINN
Chocolate Factory
3400 Phinney Avenue Nort
Seattle, WA 98103
206.632.5100
www.theochocolate.cor

Theo Chocolate
Seattle, Washington

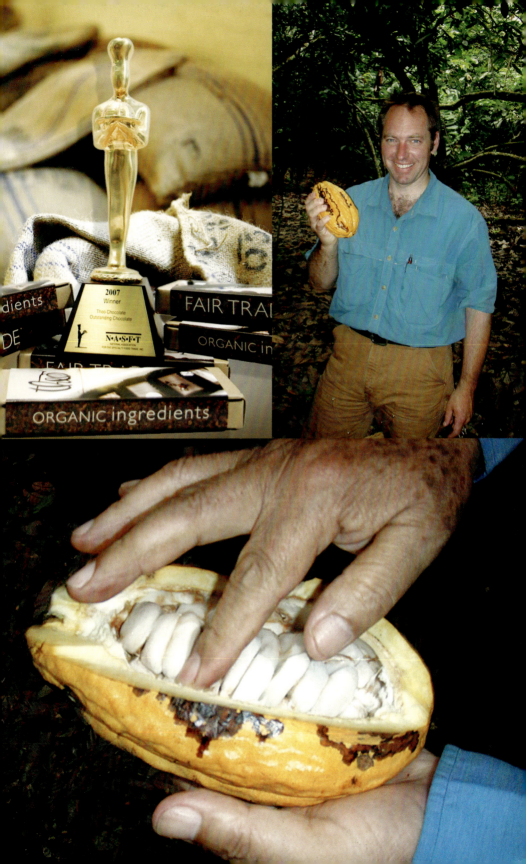

Sans Souci Gourmet Confections
PO Box 143
Olympia, WA 98506
631.331.4208
www.sanssouciconfections.net

Verdun Fine Chocolate
421 NW 10th AVE
Portland, OR 97209
503.525.9400
www.verdunchocolates.com

Telluride Truffles
Telluride, CO
866.543.0108
www.telluridetruffle.com

Sweet Ohana Candy Factory & Grill
Kailua Kona, HI 96740-1715
808.329.9676
www.sweetohanacandy.com

All photographs courtesy of each company listed above

Seattle Chocolate
Company
1180 Andover Park W
Seattle, WA 98188
seattlechocolates.com

Michele's Chocolate
14698 SE 82nd Dr.
Clackamas, OR 97015
800.656.7112
www.micheles.com

AvenueSweets
PO Box 521620
Salt Lake City, Utah 84152
www.avenuesweets.com

Gosanko Chocolate Art
116 'A' Street Southeast
Auburn, WA 98002
253.333.7567
www.gosankochocolate.com

The Chocolate Suite
by Cocoa West Chocolatier
Bowen Island, BC, Canada

Images by Cocoa West and Marilyn Gillespie

The Chocolate Suite

Created by Cocoa West Chocolatier, the Chocolate Suite is a 'bed and chocolate' retreat on Canada's Bowen Island, and is inspired by a passion for fine organic chocolate truffles and exotic hot chocolate. The Chocolate Suite design includes a private entrance, dining nook, sitting area, bathroom featuring rain-head shower and natural pebble floor, film & book selection, mood lighting, and a selection of Cocoa West's organic chocolates.

Terra Nostra™
Organic Chocolate

2385 Burrard St.   Vancouver BC V6J 3J2 Canada 888.439.4443
www.terranostrachocolate.com

Terra Nostra is a manufacturer of some of the best tasting organic chocolates; infused with chocolate magic, created by a master chocolatier, and taste tested by two divas and a British critic. Its products are known in the industry for their magnificent taste, silky texture, and consistent quality. A small but intent company, it executes sustainable chocolate production while creating new & exciting flavour profiles to challenge and entice the palate, such as their chocolate bar with Goji Berries & Pink Himalayan Mineral Salt. Terra Nostra also has a line of Ricemilk Choco™ bars for those who are lactose intolerant or follow a vegan diet but are missing the pleasure of chocolate.

Awarded by the International Taste & Quality Institute in Brussels, Terra Nostra™ Organic is devoted to the balance between decadence, superior quality organic chocolate & sustainability. It seeks to challenge the chocolate industry by creating bars that maintain the highest standards in taste and the quality of its ingredients while remaining firm in its message for ethical profit through initiatives such as Equitable Trade as well as with Sustainable Harvest International. Terra Nostra Organic offsets 100% of its carbon emissions created by its US chocolate bar production through the purchase of wind power RECs (Renewable Energy Credits) from Clean and Green and is third party certified by Green-e. The RECs are bought directly from community based wind farms, allowing the profits to be maintained and re-invested to build more infrastructure that increments the production of renewable Green-e energy.

Terra Nostra's organic chocolate bar line was created by fifth generation chocolatier, Karlo Flores, who states that his mission is to create a better planet for our children through his passion for chocolate. Says Karlo: I started making Organic chocolate as a response to the overwhelming feeling of responsibility I had 3 months before my son was born. I wanted to leave him with a chance at a better world, feed him the most natural food, and Organic was my answer to this spiritual need.

Where to buy: Located at most Whole Foods Markets but please visit the store locator for a retailer near you at www.terranostarchocolate.com or you can buy directly from the Terra Nostra on-line store.

TERRA NOSTRA
organic
Best Tasting Organic Chocolate

DOUBLE DARK™
TRUFFLE

60% CACAO

3.5 oz 100 g

TERRA NOSTRA
organic
Best Tasting Organic Chocolate

ROBUST DARK™
RAISINS &
PECANS

60% CACAO

3.5 oz 100 g

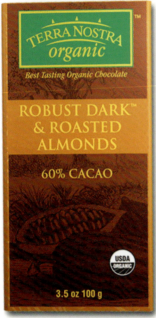

TERRA NOSTRA
organic
Best Tasting Organic Chocolate

ROBUST DARK™
& ROASTED
ALMONDS

60% CACAO

3.5 oz 100 g

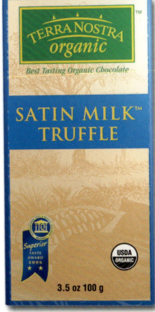

TERRA NOSTRA
organic
Best Tasting Organic Chocolate

SATIN MILK™
TRUFFLE

3.5 oz 100 g

Monde Chocolat
The World in Chocolate

2391 Burrard St.   Vancouver   BC   V6J 3J2   Canada
604.733.2462 (CHOC)   www.mondechocolat.com

Monde Chocolat is a Vancouver based chocolate boutique specializing in all things chocolate. One enters and is immediately warmed and enticed by the rich smells of fine chocolates filling the senses in every way: Chocolate fountains roll white and dark chocolate in the window and unwittingly tease the unassuming passer-by; colors by Zotter bars emulate the playful colors of the impressionistic paintings as well as bold statuesque bars

of Valrhona and Cluiziel line the walls. Monde Chocolat is an 'Ode to Chocolate' revering and honoring the authenticity of fine chocolates and bringing different varieties of rare & exquisite chocolates from around the world.

Co-Founder Fabiana Makon-Flores is the visionary, designer and buyer for Monde Chocolat. The establishment finds its inspiration from the classic European chocolaterie but differs in its format from most chocolate boutiques in that it doesn't only carry European truffles but also exclusive and highly refined bars, as well as its own in-store made signature items. Delectable choices range from barks, frozen cheesecake on a stick dipped in organic chocolate, chocolate books, and chocolate fountains to professional chocolate decorations for baking as well as alternative dietary needs chocolates. Monde Chocolat products also include ice cream dessert, signature ice cream bars, chocolate covered strawberries, Zotter Schokolade, M.Cluiziel, Valrhona, Abtey, Stella, Bernrain, Camille Bloch, Maestrani, Bon Bona, and Terra Nostra Organic's full line including the unique non-dairy Rice Milk bars.

Jean Philippe Patisserie
at Bellagio
Las Vegas
NV
(702) 693-7111

M & M's World
3785 Las Vegas Blvd S Ste 10
Las Vegas
NV
(702) 736-7611

Vosges Haut Chocolat
Forum Shops at Caesars
Las Vegas
NV
(702) 836-9866

Chocolat
Wynn Las Vegas
Las Vegas
NV

Bernard C Chocolates
440 5th St Unit A
Lake Oswego
OR

Chocolate Etc
220 A Ave
Lake Oswego
OR

Van Duyn Chocolates
12000 SE 82ND Ave Ste 1100
Happy Valley
OR

Simply Irresistible
1620 SE Bybee Blvd
Portland
OR

Debon Chocolate Cafe
900 SW 5th Ave
Portland
OR

Cacao Drink Chocolate
414 SW 13th Ave
Portland
OR
(503) 241-0656

Moonstruck Chocolate Cafe
608 SW Alder St
Portland
OR

DePaula Confections
6140 SW 41st Ave
Portland
OR
(503) 892-2462

Sahagun Handmade Chocolates
10 NW 16th Avenue
Portland
OR
(503) 274-7065

Sweet Masterpiece Chocolates
922 NW Davis Street
Portland
OR
(503) 221-0055

Moonstruck Chocolate Cafe
526 NW 23rd Ave
Portland
OR
(503) 542-3400

Wild Sweets Chocolate Factory
1412 SE Madison St
Portland
OR

Michelle's Chocolate Truffles
2209 SE Hawthorne Blvd
Portland
OR

Sweets Etc
7828 SW Capitol Hwy
Portland
OR

Paradise Chocolates
824 NW Murray Blvd
Portland
OR

Brach & Brock Confections
15939 NE Cameron Blvd
Portland
OR

Van Duyn Chocolates
1212 Lloyd Ctr
Portland
OR

Amore Chocolates & Gifts
10149 1/2 Main St
Bellevue
WA

Oh! Chocolate Bellevue Place
10500 NE 8th St Ste 8
Bellevue
WA

Fran's Chocolates
10036 Main St
Bellevue
WA

Edible Art Chocolates
20924 33rd Dr SE
Bothell
WA

Boehm's Homemade Swiss Candies
255 NE Gilman Blvd
Issaquah
WA

Oh! Chocolate Mercer Island
2703 76th Ave Se
Mercer Island
WA

Dilettante Chocolates
1603 1st Ave
Seattle
WA
(206) 728-9144

Fiori Chocolatiers
1904 Ninth Ave
Seattle
WA

Oh! Chocolate Madison
3131 E Madison St
Seattle
WA

Rose's Chocolate Treasures
1906 Post Alley
Seattle
WA
(206) 441-2936

Chocolate Box
108 Pine St
Seattle
WA

Neuhaus Chocolates
410 University St
Seattle
WA

Chocolate Co LLC
3400 Phinney Ave N
Seattle
WA

Chocolaties Chocolate Co
7708 Aurora Ave N
Seattle
WA

Heavenly Chocolates
3508 Densmore Ave N
Seattle
WA

Fran's Chocolates and Ice
Cream
2626 NE University Village St
Seattle
WA

Seattle Fudge
305 Harrison St Ste 66
Seattle
WA

Chocolate Bar
1024 Southcenter Mall
Tukwila
WA

Seattle Chocolate Co
1180 Andover Park W
Tukwila
WA

Marketplace Sweet Shoppe
8805 N Harborview Dr
Gig Harbor
WA

Monica's Chocolat Box
10225 Kopachuck Dr NW
Gig Harbor
WA

Boehm's Chocolates At
Poulsbo
PO Box 2253
Poulsbo
WA

THE CHOCOLATE GUIDE

To Local Chocolatiers, Chocolate Makers, Boutiques
Patisseries & Shops - Western Edition

tcb-cafe Publishing and media
PO Box 471706
San Francisco, California 94147
www.cafeandre.com
www.ChocolateTelevision.com